A Gift For:

From:

GOD WILL CARRY YOU THROUGH

MAX LUCADO

COUNTRYMAN

A Division of Thomas Nelson Publishers
Since 1798

THOMAS NELSON
Since 1798

NASHVILLE   DALLAS   MEXICO CITY   RIO DE JANEIRO

CONTENTS

PREFACE

It's the signature theme of the Bible: God coming to the aid of his children. Isaac's last-minute reprieve from certain death at the hand of obedient Abraham. The children of Israel rescued from the brick-pits of Egypt. Saul became Paul, liberated from a path of hatred and violence. And all the redeemed, delivered from destruction by the gift of a Savior.

Again and again, stories of heavenly oversight and divine rescue capture our imagination and help build our trust that the same God will do the same for us. In stories of old, our heavenly Father demonstrated his might with divided seas, guiding clouds, blinding lights, miraculous healings, unquenchable fires.

The same God who stepped in and rerouted history cares about our own struggles, fears, tears, and hopes. Facing financial woes, relationship dead ends, or health crises? You will get through these trials. It won't be easy or quick or painless, but God will carry you through. Trust him.

I pray that the stories in this book of brothers and sisters who've faced challenges in need of Red Sea-parting power will encourage you as you walk through your own struggles.

In their own words, these fellow travelers share their "Joseph" moments and how God carried them through. He'll do the same for you.

—Max Lucado

You'll get through this.

It won't be painless.

It won't be quick.

But God will use this mess for good.

Don't be foolish or naive.

But don't despair either.

With God's help, you will get through this.

GOD
CARRIES US
THROUGH

GOD WILL CARRY YOU THROUGH

You'll get through this.

You fear you won't. We all do. We fear that the depression will never lift, the yelling will never stop, the pain will never leave. . . . We wonder: *Will this gray sky ever brighten? This load ever lighten?* We feel stuck, trapped, locked in. Predestined for failure. Will we ever exit this pit?

Yes!

Deliverance is to the Bible what jazz music is to Mardi Gras—bold, brassy, and everywhere. Deliverance:

out of the lion's den for Daniel,
the prison for Peter,
the whale's belly for Jonah,
Goliath's shadow for David,
the storm for the disciples,
disease for the lepers,
doubt for Thomas,
the grave for Lazarus,
and the shackles for Paul.

God carries us through stuff:

through the Red Sea onto dry ground (Exodus 14:22),
through the wilderness (Deuteronomy 29:5),
through the valley of the shadow of death (Psalm 23:4),
and *through* the deep sea (Psalm 77:19).

GOD CARRIES US THROUGH

Through is a favorite word of God's:

"When you pass through the waters, I will be with you;
And through the rivers, they shall not overflow you.
When you walk through the fire, you shall not be
*   burned,*
Nor shall the flame scorch you." (Isaiah 43:2 NKJV)

It won't be painless.

Have you wept your final tear or received your last round of chemotherapy? Not necessarily. Will your unhappy marriage become happy in a heartbeat? Not likely. . . .

Does God guarantee the absence of struggle and the abundance of strength? Not in this life. But he does pledge to reweave your pain for a higher purpose.

It won't be quick.

Joseph was seventeen years old when his brothers abandoned him. He was at least thirty-seven when he saw them again. Another couple of years passed before he saw his father.

Sometimes God takes his time:

one hundred twenty years to prepare Noah for the
    flood;
eighty years to prepare Moses for his work.

3

God called young David to be king but returned him to the sheep pasture. He called Paul to be an apostle and then isolated him in Arabia for perhaps three years. Jesus was on the earth for three decades before he built anything other than a kitchen table. How long will God take with you? He may take his time. His history is redeemed not in minutes but in lifetimes.

But God will use your mess for good.

We see Satan's tricks and ploys. God sees Satan tripped and foiled.

Let me be clear ... *You represent a challenge to Satan's plan*. You carry something of God within you, something noble and holy, something the world needs—wisdom, kindness, mercy, skill. If Satan can neutralize you, he can mute your influence.

What Satan intends for evil, God, the Master Weaver and Master Builder, redeems for good.

The story of Joseph is in the Bible for this reason: to teach us to trust God to trump evil.

Good days.
Bad days.
God is in all
days.

I look up to the hills, but where does my help come from? My help comes from the LORD, who made heaven and earth. He will not let you be defeated. He who guards you never sleeps. * As the mountains surround Jerusalem, the LORD surrounds his people now and forever. * You are my help. Because of your protection, I sing. * Our help comes from the LORD, who made heaven and earth.

PSALM 121:1–3; PSALM 125:2;
PSALM 63:7; PSALM 124:8

HOPE IN THE MIDST
OF TOUGH TIMES

So it came to pass, when Joseph had come to his brothers,
that they stripped Joseph of his tunic, the tunic of many
colors that was on him. Then they took him and cast him
into a pit. And the pit was empty; there was no water in it.
And they sat down to eat a meal.

GENESIS 37:23–25 NKJV

It was an abandoned cistern. Jagged rocks and roots extended from its side. The seventeen-year-old boy lay at the bottom. At least he looked to be a boy: downy beard, spindly arms and legs. His hands were bound, ankles tied. He lay on his side, knees to chest, cramped in the small space. The sand was wet with spittle where he had drooled. His eyes were wide with fear. His voice was hoarse from screaming. It wasn't that his brothers didn't hear him. Twenty-two years later, when a famine had tamed their swagger and guilt had dampened their pride, they would confess, "We saw the anguish of his soul when he pleaded with us, and we would not hear" (Genesis 42:21 NKJV).

Joseph didn't see this assault coming. He didn't climb out of bed that morning and think, *I'd better dress in padded clothing because this is the day I get tossed in a hole.* The attack caught him off guard.

So did yours. Joseph's pit came in the form of a cistern. Maybe yours came in the form of a diagnosis, a foster home, or a traumatic injury. Joseph was thrown into a hole and despised. And you? Thrown into an unemployment line and forgotten. Thrown into a divorce and abandoned, into a bed and abused. The pit. A kind of death, waterless and austere. Some people never recover. Life is reduced to one quest: get out and never be hurt again. Not simply done. Pits have no easy exits.

Joseph's story got worse before it got better. Abandonment led to enslavement, entrapment, and finally imprisonment. He was sucker punched. Sold out. Mistreated. People made promises only to break them, offered gifts only to take them. If hurt were a swampland, then Joseph was sentenced to a life of hard labor in the Everglades.

Yet he never gave up. Bitterness never staked its claim. Anger never metastasized into hatred. His heart never hardened; his resolve never vanished. He not only survived; he thrived. He ascended like a helium balloon. An Egyptian official promoted him to chief servant. The prison warden placed Joseph over the inmates. And Pharaoh, the highest ruler on the planet, shoulder-tapped Joseph to serve as his prime minister. By the end of his life, Joseph was the second most powerful man of his generation. It is not hyperbole to state that he saved the world from starvation.

How did he flourish in the midst of tragedy? We don't have to speculate. Some twenty years later the roles were reversed, Joseph the strong one and his brothers the weak ones. They came to him in dread. They feared he would settle the score and throw them into a pit of his own making. But Joseph didn't. And in his explanation we find his inspiration:

> *As for you, you meant evil against me, but God meant it for good in order to bring about this present result, to preserve many people alive.* (Genesis 50:20 NASB)

In God's hands intended evil becomes eventual good.

Joseph tied himself to the pillar of this promise and held on for dear life. Nothing in his story glosses over the *presence* of evil. Quite the contrary. Bloodstains and tearstains are everywhere. Joseph's heart was rubbed raw against the rocks of disloyalty and miscarried justice. Yet time and time again God redeemed the pain. The torn robe became a royal one. The pit became a palace. The broken family grew old together. The very acts intended to destroy God's servant turned out to strengthen him.

"You *meant* evil against me," Joseph told his brothers, using a Hebrew verb which traces its meaning to "weave" or "plait. "You *wove* evil," he was saying, "but God *rewove* it together for good."

God, the Master Weaver. He stretches the yarn and intertwines the colors, the ragged twine with the velvet strings, the pains with the pleasures. Nothing escapes his reach. Every king, despot, weather pattern, and molecule are at his command. He passes the shuttle back and forth across the generations, and as he does, a design emerges. Satan weaves, God reweaves.

And God, the Master Builder. This is the meaning behind Joseph's words "God meant it for good in order to *bring about . . .*" (emphasis mine). The Hebrew word translated here as *bring about* is a construction term.[1] It describes a task or building project akin to the one that I drive through every morning. The state of Texas is rebuilding a highway overpass near my house. Three lanes have been reduced to one, transforming a morning commute into a daily stew. The interstate project, like human history, has been in development since before time began. Cranes daily hover overhead. Workers hold signs and shovels, and several million of us grumble. Well, at least I do. *How long is this going to last*?

My next-door neighbors have a different attitude toward the project. The husband and his wife are highway engineers, consultants to the Department of Transportation. They endure the same traffic jams and detours as the rest of us but do so with a better attitude. Why? They know how these projects develop. "It will take time," they respond to my grumbles, "but it will get finished. It's doable." They've seen the plans.

By giving us stories like Joseph's, God allows us to study his plans. Such disarray! Brothers dumping brother. Entitlements. Famines and family feuds scattered about like nails and cement bags on a vacant lot. Satan's logic was sinister and simple: destroy the family of Abraham and thereby destroy his seed, Jesus Christ. All of hell, it seems, set its target on Jacob's boys.

But watch the Master Builder at work. He cleared debris, stabilized the structure, and bolted trusses until the chaos of Genesis 37:24 ("They . . . cast him into a pit" NKJV) became the triumph of Genesis 50:20 ("life for many people" MSG).

God as Master Weaver, Master Builder. He redeemed the story of Joseph. Can't he redeem your story as well?

Lord, even when I have trouble all around me,
you will keep me alive.
When my enemies are angry,
you will reach down and save me by your power.

PSALM 138:7

Joseph would be the first to tell you that life in the pit stinks. Yet for all its rottenness, doesn't the pit do this much? It forces you to look upward. Someone from *up there* must come *down here* and give you a hand. God did for Joseph. At the right time, in the right way, he will do the same for you.

In Her Own Words:

CHARLOTTE'S STORY

For our seventeenth wedding anniversary, my husband gave me tickets to fly to Michigan to spend a week with my aunt and cousin for a "girls shopping" trip, something that I had wanted to do for several years. I flew from Florida to Michigan on our anniversary.

The next morning he dropped off our two daughters (then thirteen and fifteen years old) at church and went to the store, telling them he would be back when they got out. I was out with my cousin, aunt, and uncle when my uncle's phone rang. It was my mom: my husband had fallen, he was in the hospital, and they needed permission to perform emergency brain surgery on him. I called the hospital, gave permission for the surgery, and then rushed to the airport to get home.

God was in full control as I was able to get the next flight from Michigan to Florida. I was actually walking down the hall of the hospital as the doctor was coming out of surgery.

After my husband spent a very long month in ICU, it was clear he would not recover. He was taken off life support, and eleven hours later he joined God's choir. My daughters and I have felt God's presence with us since the minute my husband fell. Our church family had such a great impact on us during and after the ordeal.

I am very blessed to be able to say that since losing their dad, my daughters have also grown in their walk with God. All three of us have graduated from college. My older daughter is married to a wonderful godly man.

Now when I hear someone say, "God will carry you through," I am a true believer. He has brought me through— and continues to bring me through—hard times. The journey has not been easy, and tough situations aren't always resolved quickly. But God is faithful. Just lean on him.

You'll
get
through
this . . .

ONE THING
TROUBLES
CAN'T TOUCH

DON'T FORGET
YOUR DESTINY

If you and I were having this talk over coffee, this is the point where I would lean across the table and say, "What do you still have that you cannot lose?"

The difficulties have taken much away. I get that. But there is one gift your troubles cannot touch. Your destiny. Can we talk about it?

You are God's child.

He saw you, picked you, and placed you. "You did not choose me; I chose you" (John 15:16). Before you are a butcher, baker, or cabinetmaker; male or female; Asian or black, you are God's child. Replacement or fill-in? Hardly. You are his first choice.

Such isn't always the case in life. Once, just minutes before I officiated a wedding, the groom leaned over to me and said, "You weren't my first choice."

"I wasn't?"

"No, the preacher I wanted couldn't make it."

"Oh."

"But thanks for filling in."

"Sure, anytime." I considered signing the marriage license "Substitute."

You'll never hear such words from God. He chose you. The choice wasn't obligatory, required, compulsory, forced, or compelled. He selected you because he wanted to. You are his open, willful, voluntary choice. He walked onto the auction block where you stood, and he proclaimed, "This child is mine." And he bought you "with the precious blood of Christ, as of a lamb without blemish and without spot" (1 Peter 1:19 NKJV). You are God's child.

You are God's child *forever*.

Don't believe the tombstone. You are more than a dash between two dates. Don't get sucked into short-term thinking. Your struggles will not last forever, but you will.

God will have his Eden. He is creating a garden in which Adams and Eves will share in his likeness and love, at peace with each other, animals, and nature. We will rule with him over lands, cities, and nations. "If we endure, we shall also reign with Him" (2 Timothy 2:12 NKJV).

Believe this. Clutch it. Tattoo it on the interior of your heart. It may seem that the calamity sucked your life out to sea, but it hasn't. You still have your destiny.

My father had just retired. He and Mom had saved their money and made their plans. They wanted to visit every national park in their travel trailer. Then came the diagnosis: amyotrophic lateral sclerosis (ALS or Lou Gehrig's disease), a cruel degenerative disease of the muscles. Within months he was unable to feed, dress, or bathe himself. His world, as he knew it, was gone.

At the time, my wife, Denalyn, and I were preparing to do mission work in Brazil. When we got the news, I offered to change my plans. How could I leave the country while he was dying? Dad's reply was immediate and confident. He was not known for his long letters, but this one took up four pages:

> In regard to my disease and your going to Rio. That is really an easy answer for me and that is Go . . . I have no fear of death or eternity . . . so don't be concerned about me. Just Go. Please him.

Dad lost much: his health, retirement, years with his children and grandchildren, years with his wife. The loss was severe, but it wasn't complete.

Several years after Dad's death, I received a letter from a woman who remembered him. Ginger was only six years old when her Sunday school class made get-well cards for ailing church members. She created a bright purple card out of construction paper and carefully lined it with stickers. On the inside she wrote, "I love you, but most of all, God loves you." Her mom baked a pie, and the two made the delivery.

Dad was bedfast. The end was near. His jaw tended to drop, leaving his mouth open. He could extend his hand, but it was bent to a claw from the disease.

Somehow Ginger had a moment alone with him and asked a question as only a six-year-old can: "Are you going to die?"

He touched her hand and told her to come near. "Yes, I am going to die. When? I don't know."

She asked if he was afraid to go away. "Away is heaven," he told her. "I will be with my Father. I am ready to see him eye to eye."

About this point in the visit, her mother and mine returned. Ginger recalls:

> My mother consoled your parents with a fake smile on her face. But I smiled a big beautiful real smile and he did the same and winked at me.
>
> My purpose for telling you all this is my family and I are going to Kenya. We are going to take Jesus to a tribe on the coast. I am very scared for my children, because I know there will be hardships and disease. But for me, I am not afraid, because the worst thing that could happen is getting to see "my Father eye to eye."
>
> It was your father who taught me that earth is only a passing through and death is merely a rebirth.

A man near death, winking at the thought of it. Stripped of everything? It only appeared that way. In the end Dad still had what no one could take. And in the end that is all he needed.

If our hope in Christ is for this life only, we should be pitied more than anyone else in the world. * We know that our body—the tent we live in here on earth—will be destroyed. But when that happens, God will have a house for us. It will not be a house made by human hands; instead, it will be a home in heaven that will last forever. * If we accept suffering, we will also rule with him. * Praise be to the God and Father of our Lord Jesus Christ. In God's great mercy he has caused us to be born again into a living hope, because Jesus Christ rose from the dead. Now we hope for the blessings God has for his children. These blessings, which cannot be destroyed or be spoiled or lose their beauty, are kept in heaven for you. God's power protects you through your faith until salvation is shown to you at the end of time.

1 CORINTHIANS 15:19; 2 CORINTHIANS
5:1; 2 TIMOTHY 2:12; 1 PETER 1:3–5

In Her Own Words:
CINDY'S STORY

See, I have engraved you on the palms of my hands.

ISAIAH 49:16 NIV

I heard recently that if you look closely enough at the scars Jesus has on his hands and feet, you'll see your name written there. Scars indicate the site of an injury, the place where pain was experienced and blood flowed. Scars may also mean that you encountered something that could have brought death, but you survived. In that case, the mark is a permanent reminder of the second chance at life you have been given.

When my dad first told me he had melanoma, my heart sank. As a nurse practitioner, I knew that the prognosis was not good and that time was of the essence—but we serve the One who holds all time in his hands. My dad was referred to MD Anderson Hospital in Houston, but the appointment was a month away.

It was certainly the Holy Spirit who led me to pray and ask for an earlier appointment if there were a cancellation— and that was the first time I prayed aloud with my parents on the phone.

GOD WILL CARRY YOU THROUGH

Not only did God answer that prayer, but he also spoke a personal message of love by moving the appointment up to my birthday.

During all the hours of waiting for CT scans, MRIs, and ultrasounds to be performed—all of which would later have only uncertain outcomes—I would Google medical studies on melanoma. If I could just find even one case study that was like my dad's and that had a good outcome, I thought I would feel comforted. I found none.

What God did show me was the end of Isaiah 49:23— "Those who hope in me will not be disappointed" (NIV). It was as if he were asking me, "Are you hoping to find comfort in Google and the Internet, or will you allow me to comfort you?" It was so hard for me to trust because I kept wondering if I would end up being disappointed.

I had once heard *faith* defined as "confident obedience to God's Word despite the situation or consequences." Reminded of that, I decided I would just believe God. I would place my hope in him—and him alone!

On Monday, March 21, 2011—after my dad's diagnosis— we got the call that the melanoma had not spread to the lymph nodes! Praise to the One who holds our futures in his hands!

There was a period of healing, and often the recovery seemed slow—but my dad did recover!

As I write this, it has been a year since that experience.

My dad will indeed carry a scar for the rest of his life. It will always remind him of the life he could have lost but was given back. And if you look closely enough at that scar, Jesus' name is written there.

God surrounds us like the Pacific surrounds an ocean floor pebble. He is everywhere: above, below, on all sides.

GOD HAS A PLAN

His brothers . . . sold him for twenty pieces of silver to the Ishmaelites who took Joseph with them down to Egypt.

GENESIS 37:28 MSG

Down to Egypt. Just a few hours ago, Joseph's life was looking up. He had a new coat and a pampered place in the house. He dreamed his brothers and parents would look up to him. But what goes up must come down, and Joseph's life came down with a crash. Put down by his siblings. Thrown down into an empty well. Let down by his brothers and sold down the river as a slave. Then led down the road to Egypt.

Down, down, down. Stripped of name, status, position. Everything he had, everything he thought he'd ever have—gone. Vanished. Poof. Just like that.

Just like you? Have you been down in the mouth, down to your last dollar, down to the custody hearing, down to the bottom of the pecking order, down on your luck, down on your life . . . down . . . down to Egypt?

Life pulls us down.

Joseph arrived in Egypt with nothing. Not a penny to his name or a name worth a penny. His family tree was meaningless. His occupation was despised.[2] The clean-shaven people of the pyramids avoided the woolly bedouins of the desert.

No credentials to stand on. No vocation to call on. No family to lean on. He lost everything, with one exception: his destiny.

Through those odd dreams heaven had convinced him that God had plans for him. The details were vague and ill-defined, for sure. Joseph had no way of knowing the specifics of his future. But the dreams told him this much: he would have a place of prominence in the midst of his family. Joseph latched on to this dream for the life jacket it was.

How else do we explain his survival? The Bible says nothing about his training, education, superior skills, or talents. But the narrator made a lead story out of Joseph's destiny.

The Hebrew boy lost his family, dignity, and home country, but he never lost his belief in God's belief in him. Trudging through the desert toward Egypt, he resolved, *It won't end this way. God has a dream for my life.* While wearing the heavy chains of the slave owners, he remembered, *I've been called to more than this.* Dragged into a city of strange tongues and shaven faces, he told himself, *God has greater plans for me.*

God had a destiny for Joseph, and the boy believed in it.

DON'T DESPAIR,
GOD IS
NEAR

"God whispers
to us in our
pleasures,
speaks to us in
our conscience
but shouts to
us in our pain."

C. S. LEWIS

In His Own Words:
CLAY'S STORY

As a lifelong type 1 diabetic, I knew what was coming. I had seen my mother die from renal failure when she was forty-eight, and I was now forty-nine. For years my kidneys had slowly been losing function and now were down to 40 percent. I just wanted to see my only child graduate from high school. But God had other plans.

Two days before my son's graduation, I had a heart attack—and I never saw it coming! I was in great shape: I worked out five or six days a week, and I had a slim build and low cholesterol. The doctors told me, however, that years of diabetes had caused plaque to build up in my arteries. The next thing I knew, it was bypass surgery time. All the things you think are so important—job, house, graduation parties, whatever—fade into the background when you think about your chest being cracked open!

My wife and I cried as we planned for the worst and prayed for the best. I survived and began the recovery process. The dye used in the process of mapping my arteries, however, caused my kidney function to drop to 20 percent. After some days it became clear that my kidney function would keep deteriorating: I needed a kidney transplant.

While my wife was in the clinic waiting to be tested as a possible donor—and praying—Paul, the father of my son's friend, walked up to her. He put his hand on her shoulder and said he was there to be tested too. I had met Paul only a few times before. It turned out that he was a member of Journey Fellowship, a church we had visited a few times (we're now members!). And by God's grace he was an excellent match to be a kidney donor.

As weeks went by, my body was getting weaker, but my spirit stronger, as I saw the hand of the Lord on my life as he worked through countless people and in response to many prayers. I had ten medical procedures, including four surgeries in six months, and then dialysis. It culminated on December 15, 2010, with Paul and me lying in the hospital next to each other waiting for transplant surgery. We both made it through, and today our families are, needless to say, dearest friends.

The year 2010 was one of great physical pain and intense emotional distress, and while it may sound odd, I would not trade it now for anything. God drew me closer to him through all of the struggles, closer than I had been in any period of my life. Even though I had grown up in church and had been growing in my faith, the perspective I now have on life is priceless. I am so thankful for many little things every day, and I see God's beauty, love, and purpose everywhere.

You will never go where God is not.

Where can I go to get away from your
Spirit? Where can I run from you? . . . If I
rise with the sun in the east and settle in
the west beyond the sea, even there you
would guide me. With your right hand you
would hold me. * Be strong and brave. Don't
be afraid of them and don't be frightened,
because the Lord your God will go with
you. He will not leave you or forget you.
* He is not far from any of us. * The Lord
your God is in your midst, a mighty one
who will save; he will rejoice over you with
gladness; he will quiet you by his love; he
will exult over you with loud singing.

PSALM 139:7, 9–10; DEUTERONOMY 31:6;
ACTS 17:27; ZEPHANIAH 3:17 ESV

GOD IS PRESENT

*Now Joseph had been taken down to Egypt. And Potiphar,
an officer of Pharaoh, captain of the guard, an Egyptian,
bought him from the Ishmaelites.*

GENESIS 39:1 NKJV

The bidding began at the auction block of Egypt, and
for the second time in his young life, Joseph was on
the market. The favored son of Jacob found himself prod-
ded and pricked, examined for fleas, and pushed about
like a donkey. Potiphar, an Egyptian officer, bought him.
Joseph didn't speak the language or know the culture. The
food was strange, the work was grueling, and the odds were
against him.

So we turn the page and brace for the worst. The next
chapter in his story will describe Joseph's consequential
plunge into addiction, anger, or despair, right? Wrong.

"The LORD was with Joseph, and he was a successful
man; and he was in the house of his master the Egyptian"
(Genesis 39:2 NKJV). Joseph arrived in Egypt with nothing
but the clothes on his back and the call of God on his heart.
Yet by the end of four verses, he was running the house of
the man who ran security for Pharaoh. How do we explain
this turnaround? Simple: God was with him.

"The LORD was with Joseph, and he was a successful man." (v. 2)

"His master saw that the LORD was with him." (v. 3)

"The LORD blessed the Egyptian's house for Joseph's sake." (v. 5)

"The blessing of the LORD was on all that he had." (v. 5)

Joseph's story just parted company with the volumes of self-help books and all the secret-to-success formulas that direct the struggler to an inner power ("dig deeper"). Joseph's story points elsewhere ("look higher"). He succeeded because God was present. God was to Joseph what a blanket is to a baby—he was all over him.

Any chance he'd be the same for you? Here you are in your version of Egypt. It feels foreign. You don't know the language. You never studied the vocabulary of crisis. You feel far from home, all alone. Money gone. Expectations dashed. Friends vanished. Who's left? God is.

If Joseph's story is any precedent, God can use Egypt to teach you that he is with you. Your family may be gone. Your supporters may have left. Your counselor may be silent. But God has not budged. His promise still stands: "I am with you and will watch over you wherever you go" (Genesis 28:15 NIV).

You will never go where God is not.

Envision the next few hours of your life. Where will you find yourself? In a school? God indwells the classroom.

On the highways? His presence lingers among the traffic. In the hospital operating room, the executive boardroom, the in-laws' living room, the funeral home? God will be there. "He is not far from each one of us" (Acts 17:27 NKJV).

Don't equate the presence of God with a good mood or a pleasant temperament. God is near whether you are happy or not.

WHEN WE REACH TO HIM FOR STRENGTH

In Her Own Words:
SHELLEY'S STORY

Life! Just when I think I'm starting to understand and accept God's omnipotence in this pain-filled world, just when I'm starting to trust God despite the heartache I've experienced—the heartache he's allowed—I am too often tested by the evil one. You too? When I'm reading God's Word regularly, praying daily, and walking as best I can on his path of righteousness—when I've settled into a comfortable way of living out my faith in Jesus—then the roaring lion makes its presence among us known.

As a widow raising three teens on my own, I worked full-time to match the social security payment I received for the kids—and we were still short. I looked all around for resources to help fill the emptiness of having no father, and then there were matters like arranging carpools, getting kids the tutoring they needed, and dealing with occasional monetary misses. We were comfortable, I paid my bills on time, and I was at peace with having men as friends. I didn't let my insecurities send me searching for someone.

In 2001 I was working the job of my dreams when the pink slip arrived via a text on my cell phone. I was stunned!

Just a few days earlier, I had taken out a loan to consolidate my credit cards to do away with them! Tears streaming down my face, I scrambled to figure out what to do.

Then a few days later came the shock of 9-11. Kaboom! I was unemployed, I was trying to process the unprocessable 9-11, I was seeing my daughter through surgery, and I had a teenage son severely outgrowing his clothes. I guess I shouldn't have been surprised when my faith took a hit. Our family mantra had always been "We still have food in our mouths and a roof over our heads!" (This was my way of encouraging the kids to recognize God's provision for us.) Now, down on my knees, overwhelmed and fearful, I repeated the promises of God while seeking both his mercy and his guidance.

It's funny how God works in the background as our larger-than-life problems fill the foreground.

I called my boss, explained the pending surgery, and asked about my insurance. He offered to pay for three months of coverage, so I was grateful that the surgery was taken care of.

I asked God's favor as I dealt with unemployment, and I asked him to show me what to do next. A friend suggested I go to school to get whatever education would provide me some self-sufficiency. This same friend encouraged me to get an internship that would provide some financial help and then offered to fill in any crisis needs that might arise.

Semester after semester I found programs to cover the cost of school, and I graduated at the top of class.

Some families provided clothing for my son, and others periodically sent money for shoes. Life groups stepped up financially when needs overwhelmed my budget. When I reflect on that year of unemployment and other challenging years that followed, God fulfilled every single request I prayed for.

God makes this promise: Ask and you will receive! And God keeps that promise. He is faithful, and I am so proud to be his chosen one, even through each trial!

Open every
pore of
your soul
to God's
presence.

We ask you—urge is more like it—that you keep on doing what we told you to do to please God, not in a dogged religious plod, but in a living, spirited dance.

1 THESSALONIANS 4:1–2 MSG

You don't fix a struggling marriage with an affair, a drug problem with more drugs, debt with more debt. You don't fix stupid with stupid. You don't get out of a mess by making another one. *Do what pleases God.* You will never go wrong doing what is right.

DO WHAT IS RIGHT

Joseph came to have clout. He could spend and hire, send and receive. Merchants reported to him and other people noticed him. Most significantly, women noticed him. "Joseph was a very handsome and well-built young man" (Genesis 39:6 NLT). A Hollywood head turner, this guy—square jaw, wavy hair, and biceps that bulged every time he carried Mrs. Potiphar's tray. Which was often. She enjoyed the sight of him. "And it came to pass after these things that his master's wife cast longing eyes on Joseph, and she said, 'Lie with me'" (Genesis 39:7 NKJV).

The first lady of the household made a play for the Hebrew slave. . . . She courted him "day by day" (v. 10). He had plenty of opportunities to consider the proposition. And reasons to accept it.

Wasn't she married to his master? And wasn't he obligated to obey the wishes of his owner, even if the wish was clandestine sex?

Powerful Potiphar had his pick of women. His wife was likely a jaw-dropper. Joseph didn't lose his manly urges when he lost his coat of many colors. A few moments in the arms of an attractive, willing lover? Joseph could use some relief.

Didn't he deserve some? These were lonely days: rejected by his family, twice bought and sold like livestock, far from home, far from friends. And the stress of managing Potiphar's household. Overseeing the terraced gardens and multitude of slaves. Mastering the peculiar protocol of official events. Joseph's job was draining. He could have justified his choice.

Can we talk candidly for a moment? Egypt can be a cruddy place. No one disagrees with that. But Egypt can also be the petri dish for brainless decisions. Don't make matters worse by doing something you'll regret.

Joseph went on high alert. When Mrs. Potiphar dangled the bait, "he refused" (v. 8). He gave the temptress no time, no attention, no chitchat, no reason for hope. "He did not heed her, to lie with her or to be with her" (v. 10). When her number appeared on his cell phone, he did not answer. When she texted a question, he didn't respond. When she entered his office, he exited. He avoided her like the poison she was.

"[Potiphar] has committed all that he has to my hand" he announced (v. 8). To lie with her was to sin against his master. How rare this resolve. In a culture that uses phrases like "consenting adults" and "sexual rights," we forget how immorality destroys the lives of people who aren't in the bedroom.

Actions have consequences. Joseph placed his loyalty above lusts. He honored his master.

And his *Master.* Joseph's primary concern was the preference of God. "How . . . can I do this great wickedness, and sin against God?" (v. 9).

The lesson we learn from Joseph is surprisingly simple: *do what pleases God.* Your coworkers want to add a trip the gentleman's club to the evening agenda. What do you do? *Do what pleases God.* Your date invites you to conclude the evening with drinks at his apartment. How should you reply? *Do what pleases God.* Your friends hand you a joint of marijuana to smoke; your classmates show you a way to cheat; the Internet provides pornography to watch—ask yourself the question: How can I please God? "Do what is right as a sacrifice to the LORD and trust the LORD" (Psalm 4:5).

"My true brother and sister and mother are those who do what my Father in heaven wants." * I will not be afraid, because the LORD is with me. People can't do anything to me. * "I will not leave you all alone like orphans; I will come back to you. . . . Those who know my commands and obey them are the ones who love me, and my Father will love those who love me. I will love them and show myself to them." * Finally, be strong in the Lord and in his great power.

MATTHEW 12:50; PSALM 118:6; JOHN
14:18, 21; EPHESIANS 6:10

In Her Own Words:
JUANITA'S STORY

Losing your best friend, the father of your children, your husband—that's what happened to me on May 5, 2006. And grieving has to be the hardest thing to do in life. But having God on your side makes the experience truly amazing.

I lost my husband to liver disease sixteen years after his first transplant in 1990. By 2006 he needed a second liver transplant as well as a kidney transplant. When he died, my family, my friends, and, most important, God saw me through the darkness of grief. Fifty years old at the time, I was working in the medical field as a medical assistant. Unsettled at first and for the next couple of years, I was very blessed to have adult children by my side, and I found great solace in God and in the church. And he enabled me to return to college and complete my degree in nursing.

As I write this, six years after my husband's passing, I smile to see that there is still life in me. I know, however, that there is no way I could have walked this journey alone. I needed God, and he was there for me.

You've probably heard it said: God is the answer. I'm here to say it's true. God embraces me with his grace, he loves me, and he guides me. I moved to a new city where I am starting a new life. Soon after my husband passed, I felt like a tumbleweed just rolling along. Every once in a while my feet touched the ground, and the burden of grief and change got to be too much. In those times, God carried me. Just as my heavenly Father carried me, he will do the same for you. When life's burdens are too heavy to bear, trust him. You are the Lord's treasure.

It won't be painless. It won't be quick.

STRUGGLES
PREPARE US
FOR LIFE

DOES THIS STRUGGLE
SERVE A PURPOSE?

On November 28, 1965, the fighter plane of Howard Rutledge exploded under enemy fire. He parachuted into the hands of the North Vietnamese Army and was promptly placed in the "Heartbreak Hotel," one of the prisons in Hanoi.

When the door slammed and the key turned in that rusty, iron lock, a feeling of utter loneliness swept over me. I lay down on that cold cement slab in my 6 x 6' prison. The smell of human excrement burned my nostrils. A rat, large as a small cat, scampered across the slab beside me. The walls and floors and ceilings were caked with filth. Bars covered a tiny window high above the door. I was cold and hungry; my body ached from the swollen joints and sprained muscles. . . .

It's hard to describe what solitary confinement can do to unnerve and defeat a man. You quickly tire of standing up or sitting down, sleeping or being awake. There are no books, no paper or pencils, no magazines or newspapers. The only colors you see are drab gray and dirty brown. Months or years may go by when you don't see the sunrise or the moon, green grass or flowers. You are locked in, alone and silent in your filthy little cell breathing stale, rotten air and trying to keep your sanity.[3]

Howard Rutledge came to appreciate his time as a POW in Vietnam. He wrote:

During those long periods of enforced reflection, it became so much easier to separate the important from the trivial, the worthwhile from the waste. . . . My hunger for spiritual food soon outdid my hunger for a steak. . . . I wanted to know about the part of me that will never die. . . . I wanted to talk about God and Christ and the church. . . . It took prison to show me how empty life is without God.

On August 31, after twenty-eight days of torture, I could remember I had children but not how many. I said Phyllis's name over and over again so I would not forget. I prayed for strength. It was on that twenty-eighth night I made God a promise. If I survived this ordeal, the first Sunday back in freedom I would take Phyllis and my family to their church and . . . confess my faith in Christ and join the church. This wasn't a deal with God to get me through that last miserable night. It was a promise made after months of thought. It took prison and hours of painful reflection to realize how much I needed God and the community of believers. After I made God that promise, again I prayed for strength to make it through the night.

When the morning dawned through the crack in the bottom of that solid prison door, I thanked God for his mercy.[4]

Few of us will ever face the austere conditions of a POW camp. Yet to one degree or another, we all spend time behind bars.

- My e-mail today contains a prayer request for a young mother just diagnosed with lupus. Incarcerated by bad health.
- I had coffee yesterday with a man whose wife battles depression. He feels stuck (chain number one) and guilty for feeling stuck (chain number two).
- After a half century of marriage, a friend's wife began to lose her memory. He had to take her car keys away so she wouldn't drive. He has to stay near so she won't fall. They had hopes of growing

old together. They still may, but only one of them will know the day of the week.

Each of these individuals wonders, *Where is heaven in this story? Why would God permit such imprisonment? Does this struggle serve any purpose?*

Every day God tests us through people, pain, or problems. Stop and consider your circumstances. Can you identify the tests of today? Snarling traffic? Threatening weather? Aching joints?

Don't see your struggle as an interruption to life but as preparation for life. No one said the road would be easy or painless. But God will use your mess for something good. "This trouble you're in isn't punishment; it's *training*, the normal experience of children. . . . God is doing what *is* best for us, training us to live God's holy best" (Hebrews 12:8, 10 MSG).

God is at work
in each of us,
whether we
know it or not,
whether we
want it or not.

[God] takes no pleasure in making life hard, in throwing roadblocks in the way. * God began doing a good work in you, and I am sure he will continue it until it is finished when Jesus Christ comes again. * I pray that the God of peace will give you every good thing you need so you can do what he wants. . . . I pray that God will do in us what pleases him, through Jesus Christ, and to him be glory forever and ever. * For . . . when your faith is tested, your endurance has a chance to grow. So let it grow, for when your endurance is fully developed, you will be perfect and complete, needing nothing.

LAMENTATIONS 3:33 MSG; PHILIPPIANS 1:6; HEBREWS 13:20–21; JAMES 1:3–4 NLT

In Her Own Words:
DINA'S STORY

My husband and I had only been married two months when we found out I was pregnant. On my birthday we found out the baby was a boy. We also learned that not only did he have a heart defect, but there was a high probability of Down syndrome as well. We broke down and cried that day, harder than we'd ever cried. But we decided against amniocentesis, a test that might have confirmed the prognosis, and we left the health of our baby in God's hands.

Christian Coover was born on November 14, 2011. He was born with Down syndrome; with an AV (atrioventricular) canal defect in his heart, which we had been told about; and an aortic heart defect that doctors had not seen in the ultrasounds. Most babies with chromosome problems are born premature and small. Christian, however, was born full-term at 8.2 pounds and 21 inches.

Our baby boy was taken in for emergency open-heart surgery the second day after he was born, and recovery was supposed to be about three days. Instead, we spent two months in ICU. Later we found out the doctors had never seen this combination of heart defects. During that time I prayed so fervently knowing that God would heal my baby. I just knew my son would be a miracle baby.

While Christian was in the hospital, many people were praying for him. My mom used to remind me that "Christian has many people on their knees before God." But because of all the medication and his condition, his kidneys stopped working. There was nothing else the doctors could do for him. God decided not to answer my prayer the way I had hoped he would. Christian passed away on January 11, 2012.

Losing our baby didn't seem normal to me. It's the most difficult thing my husband and I have been through. I still don't fully understand why God did not answer our prayers for healing. Why even pray if God is still going to do whatever he wants to do? Clearly, my faith had never been tested like this before. At times the pain was so great that I doubted God's very existence. I lost my baby and, with him, a lot of my dreams.

But I have come to understand that Christian belonged to God, not to me. And I believe we have to *trust* that God does what is best for us. I also see that God answered my prayer for Christian's healing by restoring his little body in heaven, which is a far better place than anywhere on this earth.

We still miss our baby very much, but we firmly believe there was a reason for Christian to be with us for those two months. Christian's story has given us the opportunity to talk to others who have, at times, felt the way we felt. My husband and I also believe that by God's grace we will get through this and one day we will be with both our Lord and our little angel in heaven.

JOSEPH IN . . . BOOT CAMP?

Then Joseph's master took him and put him into the
prison, a place where the king's prisoners were confined.
And he was there in the prison. But the LORD was with
Joseph and showed him mercy, and He gave him favor in
the sight of the keeper of the prison. . . . Whatever [Joseph]
did, the LORD made it prosper.

GENESIS 39:20–21, 23 NKJV

If Mrs. Potiphar couldn't flirt Joseph into her
bed, she would force him. She grabbed for his robe, and he
let her have it. He chose his character over his coat. When he
ran, she concocted a story. When Potiphar came home, she
was ready with her lie and Joseph's coat as proof. Potiphar
charged Joseph with sexual assault and locked him in jail.

Not a prison in the modern sense but a warren of under-
ground, windowless rooms with damp floors, stale food,
and bitter water. Guards shoved him into the dungeon and
slammed the door. Joseph leaned his back against the wall,
slid to the floor. "I have done nothing here that they should
put me into the dungeon" (Genesis 40:15 NKJV).

Joseph had done his best in Potiphar's house. He had
made a fortune for his employer. He had kept his chores
done and room tidy. He had adapted to a new culture. He

had resisted the sexual advances. But how was he rewarded? A prison sentence with no hope of parole.

Why didn't God keep Joseph out of prison? Might this be the answer? "For . . . when your faith is tested, your endurance has a chance to grow. So let it grow, for when your endurance is fully developed, you will be perfect and complete, needing nothing" (James 1:3–4 NLT).

"And the keeper of the prison committed to Joseph's hand all the prisoners who were in the prison; whatever they did there, it was his doing" (Genesis 39:22 NKJV). Talk about a crash course in leadership! Joseph managed willing servants for Potiphar. But in prison he was assigned unruly, disrespectful, and ungrateful men. Joseph could have cloistered himself in a corner and mumbled, "I've learned my lesson. I'm not running anything for anybody." But he didn't complain, didn't criticize. He displayed a willing spirit with the prisoners.

God wasn't finished. Both the baker and the butler were troubled by dreams. Both men sought the counsel of Joseph. And Joseph received an interpretation from God. Would he share it? The last time Joseph spoke of dreams, he ended up in a dry cistern. Besides, only 50 percent of his revelation was good news. Could Joseph be trusted to share God's news? If called to stand before Pharaoh, would Joseph accurately convey God's word? This was a test. Joseph passed it. He gave the butler good news ("You'll be out in three days") and the baker bad news ("You'll be dead in three days"). One would get a new start; the other, a noose around the neck.

Test, test, test. The dungeon looked like a prison, smelled like a prison, sounded like a prison, but had you asked the angels of heaven about Joseph's location, they would have replied, "Oh, he is in boot camp."

> They bruised [Joseph's] feet with fetters
> and placed his neck in an iron collar.
> Until the time came to fulfill his word,
> the LORD tested Joseph's character.

PSALM 105:18–19 NLT

If you see your troubles as nothing more than isolated hassles and hurts, you'll grow bitter and angry. Yet if you see your troubles as tests used by God for his glory and your maturity, then even the smallest of incidents takes on significance.

Every challenge, large or small, can equip you for a future opportunity.

The LORD will not turn back until he fully accomplishes the purposes of his heart.

JEREMIAH 30:24 NIV

There is nothing trite about your wheelchair, empty pantry, or aching heart. These are uphill, into-the-wind challenges you are facing. They are not easy.

But nor are they random. God is not *sometimes* sovereign. He is not *occasionally* victorious. He does not occupy the throne one day and vacate it the next. This season in which you find yourself may puzzle you, but it does not bewilder God. He can and will use it for his purpose.

GOD
IS IN ALL
DAYS

STAY FOCUSED ON GOD

"Be still, and know that I am God" (Psalm 46:10 NKJV) reads the sign on God's waiting room wall.

You can be glad because God is good.

You can be still because he is active.

You can rest because he is busy. . . .

To wait, biblically speaking, is not to assume the worst, worry, fret, make demands, or take control. Nor is waiting inactivity. It is a sustained effort to stay focused on God through prayer and belief. To wait is to "rest in the LORD, and wait patiently for Him; . . . not fret" (Psalm 37:7 NKJV).

> *Those who wait on the LORD*
> *Shall renew their strength;*
> *They shall mount up with wings like eagles,*
> *They shall run and not be weary,*
> *They shall walk and not faint.*
> ISAIAH 40:31 NKJV

Fresh strength. Renewed vigor. Legs that don't grow weary. Delight yourself in God, and he will bring rest to your soul.

In Her Own Words:

GLENDA'S STORY

I had been married for twenty-five years and was the mother of three children. Then, in 1996, life as I knew it in Little Rock, Arkansas, ceased. The divorce was mutual, but hurtful because of his infidelity. I felt a strange kind of freedom and peace when he moved to Tennessee with his new wife. Little did I know the sorrow and despair I would soon face. Our two older children were grown and well on their way in life. Our youngest daughter Heather was thirteen. We shared court-ordered custody: she was to live with me and have visitations with her father.

In June 1998 Heather's father picked her up for a three-week visit. She and I had decided to make a new and better life for ourselves by moving to Texas after she returned. But two days before her scheduled return Heather called me. I could tell she had been crying. She told me she was staying with her father. He had convinced her that a better life was with his new family, not with me.

I couldn't breathe as I slumped down to the floor. Heather told me that she loved me and that she would be there in a couple of days to retrieve her things. The next morning at 7:00 my doorbell rang, and I was handed a summons to appear in court: her father and his new wife wanted full custody of my child. I knew they were doing this out of spite, and I also knew that I could not face him when he moved her out of my house. So I moved on to Texas without Heather. My pride and my hurt guided that decision.

Four years passed without much conversation because Heather felt I had abandoned her. She wouldn't answer my phone calls, or she'd make some hateful remark before she hung up. The pain overwhelmed me, and I despised myself. I had missed out on seeing my child go on her first date and learn to drive. I hadn't been able to share all the wonderful "firsts" that we parents witness. And I could no longer hug her. I blamed myself for all of this.

Soon after she graduated from high school, Heather joined the Navy. I knew then that she was gone from me for good. I hadn't turned to God up to this point, and I didn't then either. And instead of turning to him, I went down a dark, sin-filled road in an effort to avoid him. But the pain of my sin became unbearable. I got on my knees and asked God to forgive me, and then I forgave myself. Then I felt the love of God fall upon me and enfold me. A new, whole life was now possible. My joy was back.

Then one afternoon the phone rang. I heard a familiar voice say, "Mom, I want to come home." Heather was leaving the Navy. Two days later I hugged my daughter for the first time in four years. That was 2002. God heard my cries and sent Heather home to me. Now, ten years later, God has blessed me with a wonderful son-in-law and three beautiful grandbabies. My daughter gave her life to the Lord and was baptized. Heather and I hug each other a lot now. God carried both of us through a rough and painful four years.

*Whatever we may have to go through now
is less than nothing compared with the
magnificent future God has planned for us.*

ROMANS 8:18 PHILLIPS

What is coming will make sense of what is happening. Let God finish his work. Let the composer complete his symphony. The forecast is simple. Good days. Bad days. But God is in *all* days. He is the Lord of the famine and the feast, and he uses both to accomplish his will.

WAITING

"Remember me when it is well with you, and please show kindness to me; make mention of me to Pharaoh, and get me out of this house. . . . I have done nothing here that they should put me into the dungeon. . . ." Yet the chief butler did not remember Joseph, but forgot him. Then it came to pass, at the end of two full years, that Pharaoh had a dream.

GENESIS 40:14–15, 23; 41:1 NKJV

Two years! Twenty-four months of silence. One hundred and four weeks of waiting. Seven hundred and ninety days of wondering. Two thousand one hundred and ninety meals alone. Seventeen thousand five hundred and twenty hours of listening for God yet hearing nothing but silence.

Plenty of time to grow bitter, cynical, angry. Folks have given up on God for lesser reasons in shorter times.

Not Joseph. On a day that began like any other, he heard a stirring at the dungeon entrance. Loud, impatient voices demanded, "We are here for the Hebrew! Pharaoh wants the Hebrew!" Joseph looked up from his corner to see the prison master, white faced and stammering. "Get up! Hurry, get up!" Two guards from the court were on his heels. Joseph remembered them from his days in Potiphar's service. They took him by the elbows and marched him out of the hole. He squinted at the brilliant sunlight. They walked him across a courtyard into a room. Attendants flocked around him. They removed his soiled clothing, washed his body, and shaved his beard. They dressed him in a white robe and new sandals. The guards reappeared and walked him into the throne room.

And so it was that Joseph and Pharaoh looked into each other's eyes for the first time.

The king hadn't slept well the night before. Dreams troubled his rest. He had heard of Joseph's skill. "They say you can interpret dreams. My counselors are mute as stones. Can you help me?"

Joseph's last two encounters didn't end so well. Mrs. Potiphar lied about him. The butler forgot about him. In both cases, Joseph mentioned the name of God. Perhaps he should hedge his bets and keep his faith under wraps.

He didn't. "Not I, but God. God will set Pharaoh's mind at ease" (Genesis 41:16 MSG).

Joseph emerged from his prison cell bragging on God. Jail time didn't devastate his faith; it deepened it.

And you? You aren't in prison, but you may be *in*fertile or *in*active or *in* limbo or *in* between jobs or *in* search of health, help, a house, or a spouse. Are you in God's waiting room? If so, here is what you need to know: *While you wait, God works.*

"My Father is always at his work," Jesus said (John 5:17 NIV). God never twiddles his thumbs. He never stops. He takes no vacations. He rested on the seventh day of creation but got back to work on the eighth and hasn't stopped since. Just because you are idle, don't assume God is.

This season in which you find yourself may puzzle you, but it does not bewilder God.

In Her Own Words:
JENNIFER'S STORY

God definitely carried me through one of the most challenging years of my life.

I had grown up in the church and gone to church camp every summer, so I had heard many testimonies of how the Lord used different situations and trials in people's lives to make them who they were today. I prayed that the Lord would give me a story—and little did I know what he would do in response to that prayer!

I had finished my first semester in college and gone home for Christmas break. I went to the dermatologist for an infection on my face and mentioned that I had a mole on my foot. And it was a good thing I mentioned that mole: two weeks later I got the call that I had stage-four malignant melanoma. The cancer became more real when I had to find a surgeon, a plastic surgeon, and an oncologist in just one week. Then after two surgeries, I not only had to learn how to walk again, but then I began a year of chemo.

As I write this, I am almost seven years cancer-free! It is amazing to look back and praise the Lord for healing me. My scars remind me every day of that painful time, but I choose to embrace what he's done because I wouldn't be who I am today if I hadn't faced that disease. My scars also remind me of his scars and what he sacrificed so that we would have life and have it to the fullest!

It is good that one should hope and wait quietly for the salvation of the Lord. * In my distress, I said, "God cannot see me!" But you heard my prayer when I cried out to you for help. * "In this world you will have trouble. But take heart! I have overcome the world." * I waited patiently for the Lord. He turned to me and heard my cry. * Be joyful because you have hope. Be patient when trouble comes, and pray at all times. * We must not become tired of doing good. We will receive our harvest of eternal life at the right time if we do not give up.

LAMENTATIONS 3:26 NKJV; PSALM
31:22; JOHN 16:33 NIV; PSALM 40:1;
ROMANS 12:12; GALATIANS 6:9

GOOD
FROM LIFE'S
MESSES

GOD'S MATH WORKS
DIFFERENTLY

Two years out of West Point, Lieutenant Sam Brown was on his first tour of duty in Afghanistan when an improvised explosive device turned his Humvee into a Molotov cocktail. He doesn't remember how he got out of the truck. He does remember rolling in the sand, slapping dirt on his burning face, running in circles, and finally dropping to his knees. He lifted flaming arms to the air and cried, "Jesus, save me!"

In Sam's case the words were more than a desperate scream. He was a devoted believer in Jesus Christ. Sam was calling on his Savior to take him home. He assumed he would die.

But death did not come. His gunner did. With bullets flying around them, he helped Sam reach cover. Crouching behind a wall, Sam realized that bits of his clothing were fusing into his skin. He ordered the private to rip his gloves off his burning flesh. The soldier hesitated, then pulled. With the glove came pieces of his hands. Brown winced at what was the first of thousands of moments of pain.

When vehicles from another platoon reached them, they loaded the wounded soldier into a truck. Before Sam passed out, he caught a glimpse of his singed face in the mirror. He didn't recognize himself.

That was September 2008. By the time I met him three years later, he had undergone dozens of painful surgeries. Dead skin had been excised and healthy skin harvested and grafted. The pain chart didn't have a number high enough to register the agony he felt.

Yet, in the midst of the horror, beauty walked in. Dietitian Amy Larsen. Since Sam's mouth had been reduced to the size of a coin, Amy monitored his nutrition intake. He remembers the first time he saw her. Dark hair, brown eyes. Nervous. Cute. More important, she didn't flinch at the sight of him.

After several weeks he gathered the courage to ask her out. They went to a rodeo. The following weekend they went to his friend's wedding. During the three-hour drive Amy told Sam how she had noticed him months earlier when he was in ICU, covered with bandages, sedated with morphine, and attached to a breathing machine. When he regained consciousness, she stepped into his room to meet him. But there was a circle of family and doctors, so she turned and left.

The two continued to see each other. Early in their relationship Sam brought up the name Jesus Christ. Amy was not a believer. Sam's story stirred her heart for God. Sam talked to her about God's mercy and led her to Christ. Soon thereafter they were married. And as I write these words, they are the parents of a seven-month-old boy. Sam directs a program to aid wounded soldiers.

Far be it from me to minimize the horror of a man on fire in the Afghan desert. And who can imagine the torture of repeated surgery and rehab? The emotional stress has taken its toll on their marriage at times. Yet Sam and Amy have come to believe this: God's math works differently than ours. *War + near-death + agonizing rehab = wonderful family and hope for a bright future.* In God's hand intended evil is eventual good.

Are there any gods like you, Lord? There are no gods like you. You are wonderfully holy, amazingly powerful, a worker of miracles. * Lord, there is no god like you and no works like yours. * God's strong foundation continues to stand. These words are written on the seal: "The Lord knows those who belong to him." * With God's power working in us, God can do much, much more than anything we can ask or imagine. To him be glory in the church and in Christ Jesus for all time, forever and ever.

EXODUS 15:11; PSALM 86:8; 2 TIMOTHY 2:19; EPHESIANS 3:20–21

He is the Potter; we are the clay. He is the Shepherd; we are the sheep.

JOSEPH HAD AN ANCHOR

Pharaoh said to Joseph, "I had a dream, and no one can interpret it. But I have heard it said of you that when you hear a dream you can interpret it."

"I cannot do it," Joseph replied to Pharaoh, "but God will give Pharaoh the answer he desires."

Then Joseph said to Pharaoh, "The dreams of Pharaoh are one and the same. God has revealed to Pharaoh what he is about to do."

Then Pharaoh said to Joseph, "Since God has made all this known to you, there is no one so discerning and wise as you. You shall be in charge of my palace, and all my people are to submit to your orders. Only with respect to the throne will I be greater than you."

GENESIS 41:15–16, 25, 39–40 NIV

Joseph was a walking piñata. The angry jealousy of his brothers that sold him into slavery, the below-the-belt deceit by Potiphar's wife that landed him in prison, the butler's broken promise that kept him in prison. Joseph staggered but recovered. (Cue *Rocky* music.) By God's strength, he pulled himself to his feet and stood, stronger than ever, in Pharaoh's court.

Oh, the contrast. Pharaoh, the king. Joseph, the

ex-shepherd. Pharaoh, urban. Joseph, rural. Pharaoh from the palace. Joseph from the prison. Pharaoh wore gold chains. Joseph wore bruises from shackles. Pharaoh had his armies and pyramids. Joseph had a borrowed robe and a foreign accent.

The prisoner, however, was unfazed. He heard the dreams and went straight to work. No need to consult advisers or tea leaves. This is simple stuff, like basic multiplication for a Harvard math professor. "Expect seven years of plenty and seven years of famine." No one, including Pharaoh, knew how to respond. *Famine* was a foul word in the Egyptian dictionary.

The silence in the throne room was so thick you could hear a cough drop. Joseph took advantage of the pause in conversation to offer a solution. "Create a department of agriculture, and commission a smart person to gather grain in the good years and to distribute it during the lean years."

Officials gulped at Joseph's chutzpah. It's one thing to give bad news to Pharaoh, another to offer unsolicited advice. Yet the guy hadn't shown a hint of fear since he'd entered the palace. He paid no homage to the king. He didn't offer accolades to the magicians. He didn't kiss rings or polish apples. Lesser men would have cowered. Joseph didn't blink.

Again the contrast. The most powerful person in the

room, Pharaoh (ruler of the Nile, deity of the heavens, Grand Poobah of the Pyramid people) was in dire need of a scotch. The lowest person on the pecking order, Joseph (ex-slave, convict, accused sex offender) was cooler than the other side of the pillow.

What made the difference?

Joseph had an anchor. Not a piece of iron but a deep-seated, stabilizing belief in God's sovereignty.

We sense it in his first sentence: "It is not in me; God will give Pharaoh . . ." (Genesis 41:16 NKJV). The second time Joseph spoke, he explained, "God has shown Pharaoh what He is about to do" (v. 28). Joseph proceeded to inter-pret the dreams and then tell Pharaoh that the dreams were "established by God, and God will shortly bring it to pass" (v. 32).

Four times in three verses Joseph made reference to God! He locked the magnet of his compass on a divine polestar. He lived with the awareness that God was active, able, and up to something significant.

And Joseph was correct. Pharaoh commanded a stun-ning turnaround: "Can we find such a one as this, a man in whom is the spirit of God?" (v. 38). He turned the king-dom over to Joseph. By the end of the day, the boy from Canaan was riding a royal chariot, second only to Pharaoh in authority. What an unexpected rebound.

In the chaos called "Joseph's life," I count one broken

promise, at least two betrayals, several bursts of hatred, two abductions, more than one seduction, ten jealous brothers, and one case of poor parenting. Abuse. Unjust imprisonment. Twenty-four months of prison food. Mix it all together and let it sit for thirteen years, and what do you get? The grandest bounce back in the Bible! Jacob's forgotten boy became the second most powerful man in the world's most powerful country. The path to the palace wasn't quick; it wasn't painless, but wouldn't you say that God took this mess and made it into something good?

And wouldn't you think he can do the same with yours? Tally up the pain of your past. Betrayals plus anger plus tragedies. Poorly parented? Wrongly accused? Inappropriately touched? Oh, how onerous life can be.

Yet, consider this question: Is the God of Joseph still in control? Yes! Can he do for you what he did for Joseph? Yes! Might the evil intended to harm you actually help you become the person God intends you to be? Yes! Someday— perhaps in this life, certainly the next—you will tally up the crud of your life and write this sum: all good.

God will
use your
struggle
for good.

Commit your way to the Lord, trust also in Him, and He shall bring it to pass.

PSALM 37:5 NKJV

Life comes at us with a fury of flying fists—right hook of rejection, sucker punch of loss. Enemies hit below the belt. Calamities cause us to stagger. It's a slugfest out there.

Some people once knocked down never get up. They stay on the mat—beaten, bitter, broken. Out for the count. Others, however, have more bounce back than Bozo. With God's help, you can bounce back. Who knows? Your rebound may happen today.

If God can make
a prince out of
a prisoner, don't
you think he can
make something
good out of your
struggle?

In His Own Words:
RICHARD'S STORY

On August 27, 2008, an accident at work forever changed my life—for the better.

As I returned from the cafeteria with my lunch that day, the powered wheelchair I had used for over eight years abruptly stopped. Unfortunately, the forward momentum pitched me out onto the concrete sidewalk, and I broke my left femur. This accident began a journey of pain, perspiration, inspiration, and sanctification that continues on to this day.

I was in the hospital a solid nine and a half months before I was able to go home. Why so long? One reason was that I had "died" on the operating table at the end of my first surgery to repair the broken leg. The anesthesiologist who got my heart restarted visited me the next day in ICU and recommended that I avoid any and all surgeries the rest of my life. Yet due to infections and other reasons I had to undergo surgery another six times before I would get to go home.

Then after seven days at home, I rebroke my leg and had to return to the hospital for yet another surgery—the eighth one. This time an awesome orthopedic surgeon—a fellow believer—put a titanium rod in my femur. That approach seems to have finally solved my problems. I spent over eleven months—almost a full year—in various hospitals, and I was out of work for a total of fourteen months.

During that long ordeal many people asked me, "How do you keep such a positive attitude?" Some even asked, "How are you keeping your sanity?"

What kept me positive and sane was my firm belief that God has a plan for all of our lives. As a Christian I knew all along that Christ has a home for me in heaven and that since he wasn't taking me to be with him, since he continued to spare my life each time I underwent one of those surgeries, he must have a reason for me to go on living. Oh, I won't lie. Many times, too many to count, I asked myself why I kept on fighting to recover. Giving up would have been so much easier.

But God would not let me give up. For instance, he let me know how much I was loved. The great support I received from my wife and my family was amazing. Their care and prayers for my recovery helped keep me going. There was also a great group of Christian brothers and sisters who often visited me and consistently prayed for my recovery. I logged over three hundred visits from this body of believers.

So I can tell you with absolute certainty that God will carry you through whatever it is you're dealing with. God carried me through. Trust him. He will not fail you.

BEAUTY
FROM ALL
THINGS

IS GOD ALWAYS GOOD?

When the cancer is in remission, we say, "God is good."

When the pay raise comes, we announce, "God is good."

When the university admits us or the final score favors our team, "God is good."

Would and do we say the same under different circumstances? In the cemetery as well as the nursery? In the unemployment line as well as the grocery line? In days of recession as much as in days of provision? Is God always good?

For my friends Brian and Christyn Taylor, the question is more than academic. During the last year their seven-year-old daughter was hospitalized for more than six months with six surgeries for a disease of the pancreas, Brian's job was discontinued, several family members died, another was diagnosed with brain cancer, and Christyn was pregnant with child number four. Life was tough. She blogged:

> Multiple hospital stays with my daughter were exhausting, but I held faith. Losing Brian's family members one by one until there was only

one left, who was then diagnosed with stage 4 brain cancer, was incomprehensible, but I still held faith. Being hospitalized seven-and-a-half weeks with a placental abruption was terrifying, but I held faith. I held to the faith that God worked for my good, and though I did not necessarily understand the trials, I trusted God's bigger, unseen plan.

God and I had a deal—I would endure the trials that came my way as long as he acknowledged my stopping point. He knew where my line had been drawn, and I knew in my heart he would never cross it.

He did. I delivered a stillborn baby girl. With my daughter Rebecca still at home on a feeding tube and her future health completely unknown, it was a foregone conclusion that this baby we so wanted and loved would be saved. She wasn't. My line in the sand was crossed. My one-way deal with God was shattered.

Everything changed in that moment. Fear set in, and my faith began to crumble. My "safety zone" with God was no longer safe. If this could happen in the midst of our greatest struggles, then anything was fair game. For the first time in my life, anxiety began to overwhelm me.

I have spent weeks trying to figure out why a God I so love could let this happen to my family at such a time. The only conclusion I came to was this: I have to give up my line in the sand. I have to offer my entire life, every minute portion of it, to God's control regardless of the outcome.

My family is in God's hands. No lines have been drawn, no deals made, I have given our lives to the Lord. Peace has entered where panic once resided, and calmness settled where anxiety once ruled.

At some point we all stand at this intersection. Is God good when the outcome is not? Our choice comes down to this: trust God or turn away. He will cross the line. He will shatter our expectations. And we will be left to make a decision.

Difficult days demand decisions of faith.

In His Own Words:

GARY'S STORY

Since the very beginning of my life, God has been drawing me to himself. Through high school, college, and twenty-one years of marriage he was near me, but I pushed him away. You see, I thought I knew a better way to live—and that better way was my way. I didn't need God, "religious life," or any part of whatever people do in church.

I thank God for his patience. He let me go down my road of destruction because he knew it was the only way to bring this man, full of pride, to his knees. God knew bringing me low was the only way to get me to look up.

After twenty-one years of marriage, my wife was so sick of my thinking I knew it all, of my doing what I thought was right and not listening to anyone else, she asked me for a divorce. The unthinkable happened to me: I went through a divorce, which led to a business failure and ended up in bankruptcy. I was totally bankrupt! I had no wife, no family, no business, no money, no friends—and, worst of all, no relationship with Christ.

Why did this happen to me? I started looking for answers. And that's when God put a faithful Christian in my life. She shared with me a tape of her pastor's sermon, I listened to it, and the light went on. The next Sunday I attended church and—go figure—the pastor's sermon was called "The Husband's Role in the Marriage." God's timing is perfect. I hadn't been in church for years, but the first Sunday back, my heavenly Father had a special sermon just for me.

The following Tuesday morning, when I was on the trail for my 5:30 run, God told me to trust him with my life. I told him out loud, "You have to be 100 percent real—or I don't want any part of it." Through the years I had seen too many people play church, be religious, put on the church face. I wanted a real, personal relationship with God—or nothing.

At forty-three years old I was utterly humbled by God's grace and mercy. I repented of my sins and, by faith, accepted Jesus Christ as my Lord and Savior that very morning.

The rest, as they say, is history. I have an intimate relationship with God. He gave me a real hunger to learn his Word and his ways. He blessed me with a Christian wife that most men could only dream of—and seven grandchildren. I've had the blessed opportunity to lead four of them into a relationship with Jesus Christ, and I am confident that the other three are on their way.

Whatever you are going through, know that God will

GOD WILL CARRY YOU THROUGH

absolutely get you through it. Trust God one day at a time, even one hour or one minute at a time. He can and he will get you through whatever tough and painful circumstances you face.

108

Our light and momentary troubles are
achieving for us an eternal glory that far
outweighs them all. * I keep the LORD before
me always. Because he is close by my side,
I will not be hurt. * God is my protection.
He makes my way free from fault. * People
who do what is right may have many
problems, but the LORD will solve them all. *
How precious also are Your thoughts to me,
O God! How great is the sum of them! If I
should count them, they would be more in
number than the sand.

2 CORINTHIANS 4:17 NIV; PSALM 16:8; PSALM
18:32; PSALM 34:19; PSALM 139:17–18 NKJV

PLENTY AND PAUCITY

This is the thing which I have spoken to Pharaoh. God has shown Pharaoh what He is about to do. Indeed seven years of great plenty will come throughout all the land of Egypt; but after them seven years of famine will arise, and all the plenty will be forgotten in the land of Egypt; and the famine will deplete the land.

GENESIS 41:28–30 NKJV

When life isn't good, what are we to think about God? Where is he in all this?

Joseph's words for Pharaoh offer some help here. We don't typically think of Joseph as a theologian. Not like Job, the sufferer, or Paul, the apostle. For one thing we don't have many of Joseph's words. Yet the few we have reveal a man who wrestled with the nature of God.

To the king he announced:

But afterward there will be seven years of famine so great that all the prosperity will be forgotten in Egypt. Famine will destroy the land. This famine will be so severe that even the memory of the good years will be erased. As for having two similar dreams, it means that these events have been decreed by God, and he will soon make them happen. (Genesis 41:30–32 NLT)

Joseph saw both seasons, the ones of plenty and the ones of paucity, beneath the umbrella of God's jurisdiction. Both were "decreed by God."

How could this be? Was the calamity God's idea?

Of course not. God never creates or parlays evil. "God can never do wrong! It is impossible for the Almighty to do evil" (Job 34:10; see also James 1:17). He is the essence of good. How can he who is good invent anything bad?

And he is sovereign. Scripture repeatedly attributes utter and absolute control to his hand. "The Most High God rules the kingdom of mankind and sets over it whom he will" (Daniel 5:21 ESV). God is good. God is sovereign. Then how are we to factor the presence of calamity into God's world?

Here is how the Bible does it: God permits it. When the demons begged Jesus to send them into a herd of pigs, he "gave them permission" (Mark 5:12–13 NKJV). Regarding the rebellious, God said, "I let them become defiled . . . that I might fill them with horror so they would know that I am the LORD" (Ezekiel 20:26 NIV). The Old Law speaks of the consequence of the consequence of accidentally killing a person: "If [the man] does not do it intentionally, but God lets it happen, he is to flee to a place I will designate" (Exodus 21:13 NIV).

God at times permits tragedies. He permits the ground to grow dry and stalks to grow bare. But he doesn't allow evil to triumph. Isn't this the promise of Romans 8:28: "And we know that in all things God works for the good of those who love him, who have been called according to his purpose" (NIV)? God promises to render beauty out of "all things," not "each thing." The isolated events may be evil, but the ultimate culmination is good.

*I pray that the God of peace will
give you every good thing you need
so you can do what he wants.*

HEBREWS 13:20

Suppose the wife of George Frederic Handel came upon a page of her husband's famous oratorio *Messiah*. The entire work was more than two hundred pages long. Imagine that she discovered one page on the kitchen table. On it her husband had written only one measure in a minor key, one that didn't work on its own. Suppose she, armed with this fragment of dissonance, marched into his studio and said, "This music makes no sense. You are a lousy composer." What would he think?

Perhaps something similar to what God thinks when we do the same. We point to our minor key—our sick child, crutches, or famine—and say, "This makes no sense!" Yet out of all of his creation, how much have we seen? And of all his work, how much do we understand? Only a sliver. A doorway peephole. Is it possible that some explanation for suffering exists of which we know nothing at all?

PRAISE AND
THANKSGIVING

THANK YOU!

I attended a banquet recently in which a wounded soldier was presented with the gift of a free house. He nearly fell over with gratitude. He bounded onto the stage with his one good leg and threw both arms around the presenter. "Thank you! Thank you! Thank you!" He hugged the guitar player in the band and the big woman on the front row. He thanked the waiter, the other soldiers, and then thanked the presenter again. Before the night was over, he thanked me! And I didn't do anything.

Shouldn't we be equally grateful? Jesus is building a house for us (John 14:2). Our deed of ownership is every bit as certain as that of the soldier.

Thankful
people focus
less on the
pillows we lack
and more on
the privileges
we have.

I will praise you, Lᴏʀᴅ, with all my heart. I will tell all the miracles you have done. * I should put my hope in God and keep praising him, my Savior and my God. * Call to me in times of trouble. I will save you, and you will honor me. * I love the Lᴏʀᴅ, because he listens to my prayers for help. He paid attention to me, so I will call to him for help as long as I live. * Thank the Lᴏʀᴅ because he is good. His love continues forever.

PSALM 9:1; PSALM 43:5; PSALM 50:15;
PSALM 116:1–2; PSALM 107:1

*Give thanks for everything to God the Father
in the name of our Lord Jesus Christ.*

EPHESIANS 5:20 NLT

Gratitude carries us through the hard stuff.

To reflect on your blessings is to rehearse God's accomplishments.

To rehearse God's accomplishments is to discover his heart.

To discover his heart is to discover not just good gifts but the Good Giver.

CHOOSING TO BE GRATEFUL

And to Joseph were born two sons before the years of
famine came, whom Asenath, the daughter of Poti-
Pherah priest of On, bore to him. Joseph called the
name of the firstborn Manasseh: "For God has made
me forget all my toil and all my father's house." And the
name of the second he called Ephraim: "For God has
caused me to be fruitful in the land of my affliction."

GENESIS 41:50–52 NKJV

Gratitude doesn't come naturally. Self-pity does.
Bellyaches do. Grumbles and mumbles—no one has to
remind us to offer them. Yet they don't mix well with the
kindness that we have been given. A spoonful of gratitude
is all we need.

Joseph took more than a spoonful. He had cause to
be ungrateful. Abandoned. Enslaved. Betrayed. Estranged.
Yet try as we might to find tinges of bitterness, we don't
succeed. What we do discover, however, are two dramatic
gestures of gratitude.

Most parents go to great effort to select the perfect
name for their child. Joseph did.

These were the days of abundance. God had rewarded
Joseph with a place in Pharaoh's court and a wife for his
own home. The time had come to start a family. The young
couple was reclining on the couch when he reached over

and patted Asenath's round, pregnant tummy. "I've been thinking about names for our baby."

"Oh, Joey, how sweet. I have as well. In fact, I bought a name-your-baby book at the grocery store."

"You won't need it. I already have the name."

"What is it?"

"God Made Me Forget."

"If he made you forget, how can you name him?"

"No, that is the name: God Made Me Forget."

She gave him that look Egyptian wives always gave their Hebrew husbands. "God Made Me Forget? Every time I call my son I will say, 'God Made Me Forget'?" She shook her head and tried it out. "'It's time for dinner, God Made Me Forget. Come in and wash your hands, God Made Me Forget.' I don't know Joseph. I was thinking something more like Tut or Ramses, or have you ever considered the name Max? It is a name reserved for special people."

"No, Asenath, my mind is made up. Each time my son's name is spoken, God's name will be praised. For God made me forget all the pain and hurt I experienced at the hands of my brothers. I want everyone to know—I want God to know—I am grateful."

Apparently Mrs. Joseph warmed to the idea because at the birth of son number two, she and Joseph called him God Made Me Fruitful. One name honored God's mercy; the other proclaimed his favor.

In Her Own Words:
MISSY'S STORY

My story is about disappointment . . . and hope. Of fear . . . and faith.

On May 30, 2007, my children and I watched their dad, my husband, take off in his plane to go to work. As a naval aviator and federal air marshal, he traveled often, and this plane allowed him to be home sooner. As he took off, though, the engine failed, and the plane crashed into the hill in the distance. I fell to my knees crying out, "Please, God! I am not ready!"

The sheriff who came to me to deliver the news that I already knew turned out to be my former next-door neighbor and a minister at a local church. He prayed with me. Friends showed up almost immediately with food and began cleaning my home. Over the next several weeks, I was also blessed to have a friend handle the legal matters and other friends help with my four children. Two school communities poured out their prayers and love, and they donated money to my family until financial matters were settled.

At a point when certain important paperwork had to be postmarked, I was praying in the bank elevator. I wanted the process to go smoothly because I was tired and afraid of what lay ahead. The woman at the bank said she usually did not come to this particular building, but she felt as if she had "a divine mission" to fulfill. When she overheard me on the phone, she knew God had sent her to pray with me.

A message on the Christian radio station I listen to said, "If you think you cannot go one more step, know that God is there to carry you." I heard this just moments after I had pulled my car over and spoken aloud those exact words—"I can't go one more step."

Time after time, in the most difficult moments of my grief, God has blessed me so vividly that all I could do was praise him. He has been my strength from the moment the plane hit the hillside to this very moment that I write these words. It is true . . . God will carry you through.

Gratitude always leaves us looking at God and away from dread. It does to anxiety what the morning sun does to valley mist. It burns it up.

RESTORATION
AND HEALING

"IT STOPS WITH ME"

Some years ago a dear friend of mine was called to the funeral home to identify the body of his father, who had been shot in the middle of the night by his ex-wife. The shotgun blast was just one in a long line of angry outbursts and violent family moments. My friend remembers standing near the body and resolving, *It stops with me.* (And it has.)

Make the same resolve. Yes, your family history has some sad chapters. But your history doesn't have to be your future. The generational garbage can stop here and now. You don't have to give your kids what your ancestors gave you.

Let God transform you into a new person by changing the way you think.

ROMANS 12:2 NLT

Talk to God about the scandals and scoundrels. Invite him to relive the betrayal with you. Bring it out in the open.

Difficult for certain. But let God do his work. The process may take a long time. It may take a lifetime. Family pain is the deepest pain because it was inflicted so early and because it involves people who should have been trustworthy.

When they judged you falsely, you believed them. All this time you've been operating on faulty data. "You're stupid . . . slow . . . dumb like your daddy . . . fat like your momma . . ." Decades later these voices of defeat still echo in our subconscious.

But they don't have to! "Let God transform you into a new person by changing the way you think" (Romans 12:2 NLT). You are not who they said you were. You are God's child. His creation. Destined for heaven. You are a part of his family.

Don't be foolish or naive. Don't despair either.

In Her Own Words:
JESSICA'S STORY

As a child, I grew up in a wonderful Christian home. My parents took me to church, taught me about God, and instructed me to love people unconditionally. To this day, I am extremely grateful for the solid foundation for faith that God and my parents provided me. God knew that the road I would walk was going to be rough, and he was preparing me. Then he allowed me to go through a mess, so that one day I would have a message, a testimony that revealed to me as well as to others God's great glory. You see, at the young age of seven, I had my innocence ripped away from me.

That's when the sexual abuse by a family member began. Fortunately, after a year and a half, my family moved across the country. I thought that the abuse was behind me, that I could move on with my life and just forget about it. But that was not the case.

I had not told anyone about the abuse, and I wouldn't for several years. And during those years God allowed me to go through several other difficult situations, from almost drowning in class-four rapids, to being held at gunpoint in a robbery at a fast-food restaurant, being raped by a friend who had told me he was getting baptized the following week, and marrying a man who, after we got married, became verbally and somewhat physically abusive and who had relations outside of the marriage.

Through all these traumatic events, I learned to hide my feelings, my insecurities, my shame, and my pain. I had put on a mask, and I had turned away from God. No wonder I was in a downward spiral of destruction. The breaking point came when my father was diagnosed with pancreatic cancer. I immediately decided to move home to help take care of him. Nine months after the diagnosis, he passed away. God used the members of my parents' church to show me his love. God also helped me write a song for my dad's funeral, "Blessings in Tragedy."

A few months after my father's death, God prompted me to move to a new city for a fresh start in life. I have lived here two years, and God has worked in my life in major ways. I am divorced, I am going to school full-time to become an RN, and I am working full-time. God has placed certain people in my life to help me look at life from a different perspective. I now understand that, with his infinite power, God can work through the most difficult of circumstances and turn them into something beautiful.

I am still a work in progress, but I'm hopeful because I know God is not done with me. The healing transformation that needs to come after life's heartaches and pain is not easy or quick, but God *will* help us through it. I readily give him all the credit, because I know I was an absolute mess before he took hold of my heart.

God has made us what we are. In Christ Jesus, God made us to do good works, which God planned in advance for us to live our lives doing. * He who touches you touches the apple of His eye. * That person will pray to God, and God will listen to him. He will see God's face and will shout with happiness. And God will set things right for him again. * I know Jesus, the One in whom I have believed. And I am sure he is able to protect what he has trusted me with until that day. * The One who was sitting on the throne said, "Look! I am making everything new!" Then he said, "Write this, because these words are true and can be trusted."

EPHESIANS 2:10; ZECHARIAH 2:8 NKJV; JOB 33:26; 2 TIMOTHY 1:12; REVELATION 21:5

RESTORATION
MATTERS TO GOD

*Jacob said to his sons . . . "Indeed I have heard that there
is grain in Egypt; go down to that place and buy for us
there, that we may live and not die." So Joseph's ten
brothers went down to buy grain in Egypt. Now Joseph
was governor over the land; and it was he who sold to all
the people of the land. And Joseph's brothers came and
bowed down before him with their faces to the earth.
Joseph saw his brothers and recognized them, but he
acted as a stranger to them and spoke roughly to them.*

GENESIS 42:1–3; 6–7 NKJV

Initially, Joseph chose not to face his past. By
the time he saw his brothers again, Joseph had been prime
minister for nearly a decade. . . . He could travel anywhere he wanted, yet he chose not to return to Canaan.
Assemble an army and settle the score with his brothers? He had the resources. Send for his father? Or at least
send a message? He'd had perhaps eight years to set the
record straight. He knew where to find his family, but
he chose not to contact them. He kept family secrets a
secret. Untouched and untreated. Joseph was content to
leave his past in the past.

But God was not. Restoration matters to God. The healing of the heart involves the healing of the past. So God shakes things up.

"All countries came to Joseph in Egypt to buy grain, because the famine was severe in all lands" (Genesis 41:57 NKJV). And in the long line of folks appealing for an Egyptian handout, look what the cat dragged in. "So Joseph's ten brothers went down to buy grain in Egypt" (42:3 NKJV).

Joseph heard them before he saw them. He was fielding a question from a servant when he detected the Hebrew chatter. Not just the language of his heart but the dialect of his home. The prince motioned for the servant to stop speaking. He turned and looked. There they stood.

The brothers were balder, grayer, rough skinned. They were pale and gaunt with hunger. Sweaty robes clung to their shins, and road dust chalked their cheeks. These Hebrews stuck out in sophisticated Egypt like hillbillies at Times Square. When their time came to ask Joseph for grain, they didn't recognize him. His beard was shaved, his robe was royal, and the language he spoke was Egyptian. Black makeup extended from the sides of his eyes. He wore a black wig that sat on his head like a helmet. It never occurred to them that they were standing before their baby brother.

Thinking the prince couldn't understand Hebrew, the brothers spoke to him with their eyes and gestures. They pointed at the stalks of grain and then at their mouths. They motioned to the brother who carried the money, and he stumbled forward and spilled the coins on the table.

When Joseph saw the silver, his lips curled and his stomach turned. He had named his son God Made Me Forget, but the money made him remember. The last time he saw coins in the hands of Jacob's older boys, they were laughing, and he was whimpering. That day at the pit he searched these faces for a friend, but he found none. And now they dared bring silver to him?

Joseph called for a Hebrew-speaking servant to translate. Then Joseph scowled at his brothers. "He acted as a stranger to them and spoke roughly to them" (v. 7).

I'm imagining the tone of a night watchman aroused from his midnight nap. "Who are ya? Where do ya' come from?" The brothers fell face-first in the dirt, which brought to Joseph's mind a childhood dream.

"Uh, well, we're from up the road in Canaan. Maybe you've heard of it?"

Joseph glared at them. "Nah, I don't believe you. Guards, put these spies under arrest. They are here to infiltrate our country."

All ten brothers spoke at once. "You got it all wrong, Your High, Holy, and Esteemed Honor. We're salt of the earth. We belong to the same family. That's Simeon over there, that's Judah . . . Well, there are twelve of us in all. At least there used to be. The youngest is now with our father, and one is no longer living" (v. 13 HCSB).

Joseph gulped at the words. This was the first report on his family he had heard in twenty years. Jacob was alive. Benjamin was alive. And they thought he was dead.

"Tell you what," he snapped. "I'll let one of you go back and get your brother and bring him here. The rest of you I'll throw in jail."

With that, Joseph had their hands bound. A nod of his head, and they were marched off to jail. Perhaps the same jail where he had spent at least two years of his life.

What a curious series of events. The gruff voice, harsh treatment. The jail sentence. The abrupt dismissal. We've seen this sequence before with Joseph and his brothers, only the roles were reversed. On the first occasion they conspired against him. This time he conspired against them. They spoke angrily. He turned the tables. They threw him in the hole and ignored his cries for help. Now it was his turn to give them the cold shoulder.

What was going on?

I think he was trying to get his bearings. This was the toughest challenge of his life. The famine, by comparison, was easy. Mrs. Potiphar he could resist. Pharaoh's assignments he could manage. But this mixture of hurt and hate that surged when he saw his flesh and blood? Joseph didn't know what to do.

Maybe you don't either.

Your family failed you. Your early years were hard ones. The people who should have cared for you didn't. But, like Joseph, you made the best of it. You've made a life for yourself. Even started your own family. You are happy to leave Canaan in the rearview mirror. But God isn't.

He gives us more than we request by going deeper than we ask. He wants not only your whole heart; he wants your heart whole. Why? Hurt people hurt people. Think about it. Why do you fly off the handle? Why do you avoid conflict? Why do you seek to please everyone? Might your tendencies have something to do with an unhealed hurt in your heart? God wants to help you for your sake.

THE SPACIOUS
WAYS OF
GRACE

REVENGE BUILDS A LONELY HOUSE

In 1882, a New York City businessman named Joseph Richardson owned a narrow strip of land on Lexington Avenue. It was 5 feet wide and 104 feet long. Another businessman, Hyman Sarner, owned a normal-sized lot adjacent to Richardson's skinny one. He wanted to build apartments that fronted the avenue. He offered Richardson $1,000 for the slender plot. Richardson was deeply offended by the amount and demanded $5,000. Sarner refused, and Richardson called Sarner a tight-wad and slammed the door on him.

Sarner assumed the land would remain vacant and instructed the architect to design the apartment building with windows overlooking the avenue. When Richardson saw the finished building, he resolved to block the view. No one was going to enjoy a free view over his lot.

So seventy-year-old Richardson built a house. Five feet wide and 104 feet long and four stories high with two suites on each floor. Upon completion he and his wife moved into one of the suites.

Only one person at a time could ascend the stairs or

pass through the hallway. The largest dining table in any suite was eighteen inches wide. The stoves were the very smallest made. A newspaper reporter of some girth once got stuck in the stairwell, and after two tenants were unsuccessful in pushing him free, he exited only by stripping down to his undergarments.

The building was dubbed the "Spite House." Richardson spent the last fourteen years of his life in the narrow residence that seemed to fit his narrow state of mind.[5]

The Spite House was torn down in 1915, which is odd. I distinctly remember spending a few nights there last year. And a few weeks there some years back. If memory serves, didn't I see you squeezing through the hallway?

Revenge builds a lonely house. Space enough for one person. The lives of its tenants are reduced to one goal: make someone miserable. They do. Themselves.

No wonder God insists that we "keep a sharp eye out for weeds of bitter discontent. A thistle or two gone to seed can ruin a whole garden in no time" (Hebrews 12:15 MSG).

His healing includes a move out of the house of spite, a shift away from the cramped world of grudge toward spacious ways of grace, away from hardness toward forgiveness. He moves us forward by healing our past.

When you are angry, do not sin, and be sure to stop being angry before the end of the day. Do not give the devil a way to defeat you.

EPHESIANS 4:26–27

Forgiveness doesn't diminish justice; it just entrusts it to God. He guarantees the right retribution. We give too much or too little. But the God of justice has the precise prescription.

Fix your enemies? That's God's job.

Forgive your enemies? Ah, that's where you and I come in. We forgive.

In Her Own Words:
CAROLYN AND ANNA'S STORY

Twenty years ago we walked behind my husband's casket on our way to its burial place. It was—I would later realize—a farewell to the living as well as to the dead.

Anna had been my stepdaughter for ten tempestuous years, and her beloved dad was the only one who could bring us to a place of peace. After he died, I was too caught up in my own misery to miss Anna. We traveled such different roads, and our paths never crossed. Seldom did thoughts of one another even pass through our minds. But *seldom* does not mean *never*. God knew we had unfinished business. So last June he put an idea into my mind: *Maybe I'll call her the next time I'm in Houston.* Would Anna be receptive? That key moment of opportunity came—and I trembled as I left a message. I didn't know if I would receive any response.

As I was traveling home from Houston, my cell phone rang. It was Anna! She too had been hesitant about our making contact, but in the next two hours of tearful, joyful conversation, we resolved to reunite. Glory to God! Since then Anna and I have been rejoicing together and thanking God for helping us discover a deep love we have for each other.

Our family welcomed Anna back with open arms. She needed us, as it turns out—and not surprisingly, we needed her. Anna is a bottomless well of love!

Anna and I rejoice that we have found each other. God surely has returned to us all that was lost, just as he did in the story of Joseph. What seemed a hopeless chasm caused by time and circumstance has been filled with love.

THE PROCESS OF FORGIVENESS

Begin the process of forgiveness.

1. Keep no list of wrongs.
2. Pray for your antagonists rather than plot against them.
3. Hate the wrong without hating wrongdoers.
4. Turn your attention away from what they did to you to what Jesus did *for* you.

   Outrageous as it may seem, Jesus died for them too. If he thinks they are worth forgiving, they are.

God's healing includes a shift away from the cramped world of grudge toward spacious ways of grace, away from hardness toward forgiveness.

"Remain in me, and I will remain in you."
* I have been crucified with Christ; it is no longer I who live, but Christ lives in me. * "Don't judge others, and you will not be judged. Don't accuse others of being guilty, and you will not be accused of being guilty. Forgive, and you will be forgiven." * Do not be bitter or angry or mad. Never shout angrily or say things to hurt others. * Lord, tell me your ways. Show me how to live. * May our Lord Jesus Christ himself and God our Father encourage you and strengthen you in every good thing you do and say.

JOHN 15:4; GALATIANS 2:20 NKJV;
LUKE 6:37; EPHESIANS 4:31; PSALM
25:4; 2 THESSALONIANS 2:16–17

WHEN IT COMES TO
FORGIVENESS . . .

*It came to pass, when they had eaten up the grain
which they had brought from Egypt, that their father
said to them, "Go back, buy us a little food."*

*But Judah spoke to him, saying, "The man [Joseph] solemnly
warned us, saying, 'You shall not see my face unless your
brother is with you.' If you send our brother with us, we
will go down and buy you food. But if you will not send
him, we will not go down; for the man said to us, 'You
shall not see my face unless your brother is with you.'"*

*Then [Joseph] lifted his eyes and saw his brother Benjamin, his
mother's son. . . . Now his heart yearned for his brother; so Joseph
made haste and sought somewhere to weep. And he went into his
chamber and wept there. Then he washed his face and came out;
and he restrained himself, and said, "Serve the bread."*

GENESIS 43:2–5, 29–31 NKJV

God moves us forward by healing our past.

Can he really? This mess? This history of sexual abuse?
This raw anger at the father who left my mother? This
seething disgust I feel every time I think of the one who
treated me like yesterday's trash? Can God heal this ancient
hurt in my heart?

Joseph asked these questions. You never outlive the memory of ten brothers giving you the heave-ho. They walked away and never came back. So, he returned the favor. When he saw them in the breadline, he snapped at them. He accused them of treachery and threw them in jail. "Take that, you rascals!"

Isn't it good to know that Joseph was human? The guy was so good it hurt. He endured slavery, succeeded in a foreign land, mastered a new language, and resisted sexual seductions. He was the model prisoner and the perfect counsel to the king. Scratch him, and he bled holy blood. We expect him to see his brothers and declare, "Father, forgive them, for they [knew not] what they [did]" (Luke 23:34 NKJV). But he didn't. He didn't because forgiving jerks is the hardest trick in the bag.

After three days Joseph released all but one brother from jail. They returned to Canaan to report to Jacob, their father, a weak shadow of an old man. The brothers told him how Simeon was kept in Egypt as assurance they would return with Benjamin, the younger brother.

The brothers returned to Egypt from Canaan, Benjamin in tow. Joseph invited them to a dinner. He asked about Jacob, spotted Benjamin, and all but came undone. "God be gracious to you, my son," he blurted before he hurried out of the room to weep (Genesis 43:29 NKJV).

He returned to eat and drink and make merry with

the brothers. Joseph sat them according to birth order. He singled out Benjamin for special treatment. Every time the brothers got one helping, Benjamin got five. They noticed this. But said nothing.

Joseph loaded their sacks with food and hid his personal cup in the sack of Benjamin. The brothers were barely down the road when Joseph's steward stopped their caravan, searched their sacks, and found the cup. The brothers tore their clothes (the ancient equivalent of pulling out one's hair) and soon found themselves back in front of Joseph, fearing for their lives.

Joseph couldn't make up his mind! He welcomed them, wept over them, ate with them, and then played a trick on them. He was at war with himself. These brothers had peeled the scab off his oldest and deepest wound. And he would be hanged before he'd let them do it again. On the other hand, these were his brothers, and he would be hanged before he lost them again.

Forgiveness vacillates like this. It has fits and starts, good days and bad. Anger intermingled with love. Irregular mercy. We make progress only to make a wrong turn. Step forward and fall back. But this is okay. When it comes to forgiveness, all of us are beginners. No one owns a secret formula. As long as you are trying to forgive, you are forgiving. It's when you no longer try that bitterness sets in.

JESUS
TAKES CARE
OF US

In Her Own Words:
JENNA'S STORY

I became a Christian as a teenager and met my husband at college. When we were in our twenties, we served in the church and had three kids together.

But I felt that I, like Joseph, had been thrown into a well when my husband left after fifteen years of marriage and began a life that involved drugs and another woman.

No words can describe the shock, disappointment, and anger I experienced. Alone with three kids, no money, and shipwrecked faith, I felt betrayed by the one person who had been "my family." But I came to realize God never left me. As I scrambled to establish a loving home for my kids and provide them with a sense of security, I began a journey with God that I never would have experienced if not for the tragedy of my divorce.

At first I was so furious with God, but as time went on, I turned to the Bible for comfort, specifically to the psalms of David that would make me cry every time I read them. As I followed David's example and began to cry to God, he spoke to me in my pain. I can't explain this well, but I experienced a sense of grace in my life that truly brought me to my knees and transformed me.

That was nearly a decade ago. Since then I have been strong and unwavering in my faith, and I attend a great church. For years I've brought up my kids alone, relying on God, who opened the door for me to become a nurse and look after my family. I feel like Joseph in that it's been hard to raise a family alone. It's not a prison; more like a waiting room. Yet it has shaped my life in awesome ways. Being abandoned and let down, seeing life take a seemingly wrong turn—trials and tests of my faith have turned out for good.

One more word. I feel as if my story is still unfolding. Perhaps someday I will get another new beginning. Now I am not only content in who I am but I am also trusting the Lord with my life. He's proven himself faithful and I love him!

Those who find me find life, and the LORD will be pleased with them. * "The wise must not brag about their wisdom. The strong must not brag about their strength. The rich must not brag about their money. But if people want to brag, let them brag that they understand and know me. Let them brag that I am the LORD, and that I am kind and fair, and that I do things that are right on earth. This kind of bragging pleases me," says the LORD. * Wisdom begins with respect for the LORD, and understanding begins with knowing the Holy One.

PROVERBS 8:35; JEREMIAH
9:23–24; PROVERBS 9:10

OUR SOURCE OF STRENGTH

You've never seen a scene like this. The basketball player stands at the free throw line. His team is down by one point. Only a few seconds remain on the game clock. Players on both teams crouch, ready to grab the rebound. The shooter positions the ball in his hand. The crowd is quiet. The cheerleaders gulp. Again, you've never seen a scene like this. How can I be so sure? Because the player shooting the ball has never seen a scene like this.

He's blind.

Everyone else on his team is sighted. Everyone on the other team is sighted. But Matt Steven, a high school senior in Upper Darby, Pennsylvania, can't see a thing. His brother stands under the rim, rapping a cane on the basket. Matt listens, dribbles, and lifts the ball to shoot. We wonder, why does a basketball coach place a blind kid on the foul line?

The short answer? Because the coach is Matt's big brother.

The long answer began years earlier when Matt was born with two permanently detached retinas. He lost his left eye in the fifth grade and his right eye in the sixth. But even though Matt can't see, his big brother Joe has enough vision for them both. Joe spent a childhood helping Matt do the impossible: ride a bike, ice-skate, and play soccer. So when Joe began coaching the basketball team, he brought his baby brother with him as the equipment manager. Matt never practices or plays with the team. But with Joe's help he shoots free throws after every practice. Long after the team leaves, the brothers linger—the younger one at the charity line, the older one beneath the basket, tapping a stick against the rim.

And so it is that Matt, for this tournament game, is the designated free throw shooter. Joe convinced the refs and the opponents to let Matt play. Everyone thought it was a great idea. But no one imagined the game would come down to this shot.

So far Matt is 0 for 6. The gym falls silent. Joe hits the iron rim of the basket with the cane. Up in the stands Matt's mom tries to steady the video camera. Matt dribbles. Pauses and shoots. Swish! The game is tied! The screams of the fans lift the roof of the gymnasium. Finally the crowd settles down so Matt can hear the click, and the scene-never-seen repeats itself. Swish number two! The opposing team grabs the ball and throws a Hail Mary at the other basket and misses. The game is over, and Matt

JESUS TAKES CARE OF US

is the hero. Everyone whoops and hollers while Matt—
the hero—tries to find his way to the bench. Guess who
comes to help him? You got it. Joe.[6]

Big brothers can make all the difference.

Need one? You aren't trying to make a basket, but
you are trying to make a living or make a friend or make
sense out of the bad breaks you've been getting. Could
you use the help and protection of a strong sibling? Look
to heaven.

"Jesus, who makes people holy, and those who
are made holy are from the same family. So he is not
ashamed to call them his brothers and sisters" (Hebrews
2:11). Jesus, the Prince of Heaven, is your brother. He calls
for you. "Come to me, all of you who are weary and carry
heavy burdens, and I will give you rest (Matthew 11:28
NLT). And he cares for you. In him, "we have an Advocate
with the Father, Jesus Christ the righteous" (1 John 2:1
NKJV). Your Brother promises to "supply all your need
according to His riches" (Philippians 4:19 NKJV).

Let's trust him to take care of us.

"For I know the plans I have for you," declares the Lord, "plans to prosper you and not to harm you, plans to give you hope and a future."

JEREMIAH 29:11 NIV

To the degree that we believe and accept God's vision for our lives, we will get through life.

When people junk us into the pit, we will stand up. God can use this for good. When family members sell us out, we will climb to our feet. *God will recycle this pain.*

LOVE WON

Then Joseph said to his brothers, "I am Joseph; does my father still live?" But his brothers could not answer him, for they were dismayed in his presence. And Joseph said to his brothers, "Please come near to me." So they came near. Then he said: "I am Joseph your brother, whom you sold into Egypt. But now, do not therefore be grieved or angry with yourselves because you sold me here; for God sent me before you to preserve life."

GENESIS 45:3–5 NKJV

As the sons of Jacob stood before Joseph, they were the picture of pity. Accused of stealing the silver cup. Tongue-tied goatherders before a superpower sovereign. Nothing to offer but prayers, nothing to request but help. Judah told the prince their story. How their father was frail and old. How one son had perished and how also losing Benjamin would surely kill their father. Judah even offered to stay in Benjamin's place if that was what it would take to save his family. They were face-first on the floor, hoping for mercy, but they received much more.

Joseph told the officials to clear out, his translators to leave the room. "Then Joseph could not restrain himself" (Genesis 45:1 NKJV). He buried his face in his hands and began to heave with emotion. He didn't weep gently or whimper softly. He wailed. The cries echoed in the palace hallways, cathartic moans of a man in a moment of deep healing. Twenty-two years of tears and trickery had come to an end. Anger and love had dueled it out. Love had won.

He broke the news: "I am Joseph; does my father still live?" (v. 3). Eleven throats gulped, and twenty-two eyes widened to the size of saucers. The brothers, still in a deep genuflect, dared not move. They ventured glances at one another and mouthed the name: *Joseph*? Their last memory of their younger brother was of a pale-faced, frightened lad being carted off to Egypt. They had counted their coins and washed their hands of the boy. He was a teenager then. He is a prince now? They lifted their heads ever so slightly.

Joseph lowered his hands. His makeup was tear smeared and chin still quivered. His voice shook as he spoke: "Please come near to me."

They rose to their feet. Slowly. Cautiously. "I am Joseph your brother, whom you sold into Egypt" (v. 4).

Joseph told them not to fear. "God sent me here. God did this. God is protecting you" (v. 7). In today's language, "There's more to our story than meets the eye."

The brothers were still not sure who this man was. This man who wept for them, called for them . . . and then cared for them.

"Fetch your family," he instructed, "and come to Egypt." He promised to provide for them and sealed the promise with even more tears. He stood from his chair and threw his arms around his baby brother. "He fell on his brother Benjamin's neck and wept . . . he kissed all his brothers and wept over them, and after that his brothers talked with him" (vv. 14–15).

Hostility and anger melted onto the marble floor.

At about this point the brothers began to realize they were out of danger. The famine still raged. The fields still begged. Circumstances were still hostile. But they were finally safe. They would make it through this. Because they were good men? No, because they were family. The prince was their brother.

Oh, for such a gift. We know the feel of a famine. Like the brothers of Joseph, we've found ourselves in dry seasons. Resources gone. Supplies depleted. Energy expired. We've stood where the brothers stood.

We've done what the brothers did. We've hurt the people we love. Sold them into slavery? Maybe not. But lose our temper? Misplaced our priorities? You bet. Like the shepherds of Beersheba, we've sought help from the Prince, our Prince. We've offered our prayers and pleaded our cases. We've wondered if he would have a place for the likes of us. What the brothers found in Joseph's court we find in Jesus Christ. The Prince is our brother.

From your Bible, create a list of the deep qualities of God and press them into your heart. My list reads like this:

1. God is still sovereign. He still knows my name. (Daniel 12:1)
2. Angels still respond to his call. (Psalm 91:11 NKJV)
3. The hearts of rulers still bend at his bidding. (Psalm 138:4 NKJV)
4. The death of Jesus still saves souls. (2 Corinthians 3:5–6)
5. The Spirit of God still indwells saints. (Acts 2:38)
6. Heaven is still only heartbeats away. (Matthew 4:17)
7. The grave is still temporary housing. (John 5:28–29 MSG)
8. God is still faithful. He is not caught off guard. (1 Corinthians 1:8–9 NIV)

9. He uses everything for his glory and my ultimate good. (Romans 8:28)
10. He uses tragedy to accomplish his will, and his will is right, holy, and perfect. (2 Corinthians 4:8–10 NKJV)
11. Sorrow may come with the night, but joy comes with the morning. (Lamentations 3:22–23 NIV)
12. God bears fruit in the midst of affliction. (2 Corinthians 1:5–7 NIV)

We cannot always see what God is doing, but can't we assume he is up to something good?

TO BELIEVE
IS THE
HIGHEST
THING

GOD IS IN THIS CRISIS

In the days leading up to the war with Germany, the British government commissioned a series of posters. The idea was to capture encouraging slogans on paper and distribute them about the country. Capital letters in a distinct typeface were used, and a simple two-color format was selected. The only graphic was the crown of King George VI.

The first poster was distributed in September of 1939:

YOUR COURAGE
YOUR CHEERFULNESS
YOUR RESOLUTION
WILL BRING US VICTORY

Soon thereafter a second poster was produced:

FREEDOM IS IN PERIL
DEFEND IT WITH ALL YOUR MIGHT

These two posters appeared up and down the British countryside. On railroad platforms and in pubs, stores, and restaurants. They were everywhere. A third poster was created yet never distributed. More than 2.5 million copies were printed yet never seen until sixty years later when a bookstore owner in Northeast England discovered one in a box of old books he had purchased at an auction. It read:

KEEP CALM
AND CARRY ON

The poster bore the same crown and style of the first two posters. It was never released to the public, however, but was held in reserve for an extreme crisis, such as invasion by Germany. The bookstore owner framed it and hung it on the wall. It became so popular that the bookstore began producing identical images of the original design on coffee mugs, postcards, and posters. Everyone, it seems, appreciated the reminder from another generation to keep calm and carry on.[7]

You can do the same. You can't control the weather. You aren't in charge of the economy. You can't undo the tsunami or unwreck the car, but you can map out a strategy. Remember, God is in this crisis. Ask him to give you an index card-sized plan, two or three steps you can take today.

God gives
hope because
he gives us
himself. He
wants us to
know we are
never alone.

TRUST AND ACT

When you face a crisis, seek counsel from someone who has faced a similar challenge. Ask friends to pray. Look for resources. Reach out to a support group. Most importantly, make a plan.

Management guru Jim Collins has some good words here. He and Morten T. Hansen studied leadership in turbulent times. They looked at more than twenty thousand companies, sifting through data in search of an answer to this question: "Why in uncertain times do some companies thrive while others do not?" They concluded, "[Successful leaders] are not more creative. They're not more visionary. They're not more charismatic. They're not more ambitious. They're not more blessed by luck. They're not more risk-seeking. They're not more heroic. And they're not more prone to making big, bold moves." Then what sets them apart? "They all led their teams with a surprising method of self-control in an out-of-control world."[8]

In the end, it's not the flashy and flamboyant who survive. It is those with steady hands and sober minds. People like Roald Amundsen. In 1911, he headed up the Norwegian team in a race to the South Pole. Robert Scott directed a team from England. The two expeditions faced identical challenges and terrain. They endured the same freezing temperatures and unforgiving environment. They had equal access to the technology and equipment of their day. Yet Amundsen and his team reached the South Pole thirty-four days ahead of Scott. What made the difference?

Planning. Amundsen was a tireless strategist. He had a clear strategy of traveling fifteen to twenty miles a day. Good weather? Fifteen to twenty miles. Bad weather? Fifteen to twenty miles. No more. No less. Always fifteen to twenty miles.

Scott, by contrast, was irregular. He pushed his team to exhaustion in good weather and stopped in bad. The two men had two different philosophies and, consequently, two different outcomes. Amundsen won the race without losing a man. Scott lost not only the race but also his life and the lives of all his team members.[9]

All for the lack of a plan.

You'd prefer a miracle for your crisis? You'd rather see the bread multiplied or the stormy sea turned to glassy calm in a finger snap? God may do this.

Then, again, he may tell you, "I'm with you. I can use this for good. Now, let's make a plan." Trust him to help you.

God's sovereignty doesn't negate our responsibility.

Just the opposite. It empowers it. When we trust God, we think more clearly and react more decisively. Like Nehemiah, who said, "We prayed to our God and posted a guard day and night to meet this threat" (Nehemiah 4:9 NIV).

We prayed . . . and posted. We trusted and acted. Trust God to do what you can't. Obey God and do what you can.

Just as the heavens are higher than the earth,
so are my ways higher than your ways
and my thoughts higher than your thoughts.

ISAIAH 55:9

Don't let the crisis paralyze you.
Don't let the sadness overwhelm you.
Don't let the fear intimidate you.
To do nothing is the wrong thing.
To do something is the right thing.
And to believe is the highest thing.

GOD PUTS PAIN TO USE

I enjoyed breakfast recently with a friend. Most of our talk revolved around the health of his fourteen-year-old son. Seven years ago a tumor was found behind the boy's spleen. The discovery led to several months of strenuous prayer and chemotherapy. The son recovered. He is now playing high school football, and the cancer clinic is a distant memory.

The discovery of the tumor was the part of the story I found fascinating. When the boy was seven years old, he was horsing around with cousins. One of them accidentally kicked him in the stomach. Acute pain led to a hospital visit. An alert doctor requested a series of tests. And the tests led the surgeon to discover and remove the tumor. After the cancer was removed, the father asked the physician how long the tumor had been present. Although it was impossible to know with certainty, the form and size of the tumor indicated that it was no more than two or three days old.

"So," I said, "God used a kick in the gut to get your boy into treatment."

Then there is the story of Isabel. She spent the first

three and one-half years of her life in a Nicaraguan orphanage. No mother, no father. No promise of either. With all orphans, odds of adoption diminish with time. Every passing month decreased Isabel's chance of being placed in a home.

And then a door slammed on her finger. She was following the other children into the yard to play when a screen door closed on her hand. Pain shot up her arm, and her scream echoed through the playground. Question: Why would God let this happen? Why would a benevolent, omnipotent God permit an innocent girl with more than her share of challenges to feel additional pain?

Might he be calling for the attention of Ryan Schnoke, the American would-be father who was sitting in the playroom nearby? He and his wife, Cristina, had been trying to adopt a child for months. No other adult was nearby to help Isabel, so Ryan walked over, picked her up, and comforted her.

Several months later when Ryan and Cristina were close to giving up, Ryan remembered Isabel and resolved to try one more time. This time the adoption succeeded. Little Isabel is growing up in a happy, healthy home.

A kick in the gut?

A finger in the door?

God doesn't manufacture pain, but he certainly puts it to use.

God, hear my cry; listen to my prayer. I call
to you from the ends of the earth when
I am afraid. Carry me away to a high
mountain. You have been my protection, like
a strong tower against my enemies. Let me
live in your Holy Tent forever. Let me find
safety in the shelter of your wings. * Give all
your worries to him, because he cares about
you. . . . God, who gives all grace, will make
everything right. He will make you strong
and support you and keep you from falling.
* "Don't worry about tomorrow, because
tomorrow will have its own worries. Each
day has enough trouble of its own."

PSALM 61:1–4; 1 PETER 5:7, 10; MATTHEW 6:34

With God's help, you will get through this.

In Her Own Words:
BROOK'S STORY

I grew up in an amazing Christian home, and I witnessed a picture-perfect marriage as my parents guided me steadfastly to live for the Lord. I loved God, but in my youth I fell completely out of step with what it meant to live for God.

When I went to college, I drank . . . a lot. After I graduated from college, I continued to associate with people who did not publicly value the Lord. I wanted and kept looking for peace, stability, and an amazing husband . . . none of which I found.

Feeling the loneliness that comes with pursuing the things of the world, I decided to quit my job and move across the country to live in DC with my sisters. I figured close proximity to my family would help ease the ache and fill the void. Within two weeks, I met Patrick. He loved his family, the Lord, and me. We began dating, and everything about my life was looking brighter.

After we had dated for six months, though, Patrick fell ill. He was diagnosed with stage IV lymphoblastic lymphoma—a childhood cancer not generally found in adults. And that cancer was everywhere—in his lymph nodes, bone marrow, everywhere. Dates and nights on the town in DC turned to long days and nights in hospitals, where I saw the true ugliness of cancer. Our relationship became nurse and patient rather than the typical dating couple.

I cried . . . a lot. I prayed . . . a lot. But I still didn't go back to church. Furthermore, I was relying on God to get Patrick and me through this, but I wasn't praising him. I was pleading with my heavenly Father at every turn, but I wasn't trusting in the fullness of his power and grace. My sister finally called me out on that. Heather demanded that I return to the Christian lifestyle we were raised to live and begin attending church on a regular basis. Insisting that I begin walking in step with what she knew I believed, she said the only way I would get through this mess was to fully rely on the Lord.

So when Patrick was not in the hospital, he and I began attending church together regularly. We began worshiping together, which for me added a whole new dimension to our relationship. Worship also reminded me that no cancer is too big for our God. After three long years of chemo and radiation, after too many hospital visits to count, Patrick has been cancer-free for six years.

After we married, God reminded us how big he is and how he loves to see us rejoice after he has brought us through a storm. Then, against all odds and despite what seemed like insurmountable medical roadblocks, God blessed us with a child. We named her Grace.

Do you recite your woes more naturally than you do heaven's strength? If so, no wonder life is tough. You're assuming God isn't in this crisis.

He is.

GOD WAS IN THE CRISES

Now there was no bread in all the land; for the famine was very severe, so that the land of Egypt and the land of Canaan languished because of the famine.

GENESIS 47:13 NKJV

During the time Joseph was struggling to reconcile with his brothers, he was also navigating a catastrophe. It'd been two years since the last drop of rain. The sky was endlessly blue. The sun relentlessly hot. Animal carcasses littered the ground, and no hope appeared on the horizon. The land was a dust bowl. No rain meant no farming. No farming meant no food. When people appealed to Pharaoh for help, he said, "Go to Joseph; whatever he says to you, do" (Genesis 41:55 NKJV).

Joseph faced a calamity on a global scale.

Yet contrast the description of the problem with the outcome. Years passed, and the people told Joseph, "You have saved our lives; let us find favor in the sight of my lord, and we will be Pharaoh's servants" (Genesis 47:25 NKJV).

The people remained calm. A society that was ripe for bedlam actually thanked the government rather than attacked it. Makes a person wonder if Joseph ever taught a course in crisis management. If he did, he included the words he told his brothers: "God sent me before you to preserve life. For these two years the famine has been in the land, and there are still five years in which there will be neither plowing nor harvesting. And God sent me before you" (45:5–7).

Joseph began and ended his crisis assessment with references to God. He assumed God was in the crisis.

Then he faced the crisis with a plan. He collected grain during the good years and redistributed it in the bad. When the people ran out of food, he gave it to them in exchange for money, livestock, and property. After he stabilized the economy, he gave the people a lesson on money management. "Give a fifth to Pharaoh, and four fifths shall be your own, as seed for the field and as food for yourselves . . ." (47:24 ESV).

Joseph never raised the dead, but he kept people from dying. He never healed the sick, but he kept sickness from spreading. He made a plan and stuck with it. And because he did, the nation survived. He triumphed with a calm, methodical plan.

*Since we are surrounded by so great
a cloud of witnesses, let us lay aside
every weight, and the sin which so
easily ensnares us, and let us run with
endurance the race that is set before us.*

HEBREWS 12:1 NKJV

High above us there is a crowd of witnesses. They are the Abrahams, Jacobs, and Josephs from all generations and nations. . . . Listen carefully and you will hear a multitude of God's children urging you on. "Run!" they shout. "Run! God will carry you through this!"

FROM
MOURNFUL TO
HOPEFUL

WAITING FOR YOU IN HEAVEN

Colton Burpo was only four years old when he survived an emergency appendectomy. His parents were overjoyed at his survival. But they were stunned at his stories. Over the next few months, Colton talked of his visit to heaven. He described exactly what his parents were doing during the surgery and told stories of people he met in heaven—people he had never met on earth or been told about. In the book *Heaven Is for Real*, Colton's father relates the moment that the four-year-old boy told his mom, "You had a baby die in your tummy, didn't you?"

The parents had never mentioned the miscarriage to their son. He was too young to process it. Emotion filled his mother's face:

"Who told you I had a baby die in my tummy?"

"She did, Mommy. She said she died in your tummy.

"It's okay, Mommy. She's okay. God adopted her."

"Don't you mean Jesus adopted her?"

"No, Mommy. His Dad did."

"What's her name?" asked the mom. "What was the little girl's name?"

"She doesn't have a name. You guys didn't name her."

The parents were stunned. There is no way Colton would have known this. He had one more memory. He shared it before he went out to play: "She said she can't wait for you and Daddy to get to heaven."[10]

Someone in heaven is saying the same words about you. Your grandpa? Aunt? Your child? They are looking toward the day when God's family is back together. Shouldn't we do the same?

*[God] will wipe away every tear
from their eyes, and there will be no
more death, sadness, crying, or pain,
because all the old ways are gone.*

REVELATION 21:4

God's first action in heaven will be to rub a thumb across the cheek of every child as if to say, "There, there . . . no more tears." This long journey will come to an end. You will see him.

And you will see *them*.

Our final home will hear no good-byes. We will speak of the Good Book and remember good faith, but *good-bye*? Gone forever.

Let the promise change you. From sagging to seeking, from mournful to hopeful. From dwellers in the land of good-bye to a heaven of hellos. The Prince has decreed a homecoming.

A FAMILY REUNION

Joseph provided [his brothers] with wagons . . . and he gave
them supplies for the journey. And he gave each of them new
clothes—but to Benjamin he gave five changes of clothes
and 300 pieces of silver. He also sent his father ten female
donkeys loaded with the finest products of Egypt, and
ten male donkeys loaded with grain and bread and other
supplies he would need on his journey. So Joseph sent his
brothers off, and as they left, he called after them, "Don't
quarrel about all this along the way!" And they left Egypt
and returned to their father, Jacob, in the land of Canaan.

GENESIS 45:21–25 NLT

Jacob's boys returned to Canaan in style. Gone
were the shabby robes and emaciated donkeys. They drove
brand-new pickup trucks packed with gifts. They wore
leather jackets and alligator skin boots. Their wives and
kids spotted them on the horizon. "You're back! You're
back!" Hugs and backslaps all around.

Jacob emerged from a tent. A rush of hair, rangy and
silver, reached his shoulders. Stooped back. Face leathery,
like rawhide. He squinted at the sun-kissed sight of his sons
and all the plunder. He was just about to ask where they
stole the stuff when one of them blurted, "'Joseph is still

alive, and he is governor over all the land of Egypt.' And Jacob's heart stood still, because he did not believe them" (Genesis 45:26 NKJV).

The old man grabbed his chest. He had to sit down. Sadness had sapped the last drop of joy out of Jacob. Yet when the sons told him what Joseph had said, how he had asked about Jacob, how he had called them to Egypt, Jacob's spirit revived.

His eyes began to sparkle, and his shoulders straightened. "Then Israel said, 'It is enough. Joseph my son is still alive. I will go and see him before I die'" (v. 28).

Jacob was 130 years old by this point. Hardly a spring chicken. He had a hitch in his getalong, an ache in his joints. But nothing was going to keep him from his son. He took his staff in hand and issued the command: "Load 'em up! We are headed to Egypt."

The whole gang of seventy made the trip.

And what a trip it was. Pyramids. Palaces. Irrigated farms. Silos. They had never seen such sights. Then the moment they'd been waiting for: a wide flank of royalty appeared on the horizon. Chariots, horses, and the Imperial Guard.

As the entourage drew near, Jacob leaned forward to get a better glimpse of the man in the center chariot. When he saw his face, Jacob whispered, "Joseph, my son."

Across the distance, Joseph leaned forward in his chariot. He told his driver to slap the horse. When the two groups met on the flat of the plain, the prince didn't hesitate. He bounded out of his chariot and ran in the direction of his father. "The moment Joseph saw him, he threw himself on his neck and wept" (Genesis 46:29 MSG).

Gone were the formalities. Forgotten were the proprieties. Joseph buried his face in the crook of his father's shoulder. "He wept a long time" (v. 29). As tears moistened the robe of his father, both men resolved that they would never say good-bye to each other again.

Good-bye. For some of you this word is the challenge of your life. To get through this is to get through this raging loneliness, this strength-draining grief. You sleep alone in a double bed. You walk the hallways of a silent house. You catch yourself calling out his name or reaching for her hand. Like Jacob, the separation has exhausted your spirit. You feel quarantined, isolated. The rest of the world has moved on; you ache to do the same. But you can't; you can't say good-bye.

If you can't, take heart. God has served notice. All farewells are on the clock. They are filtering like grains of sand through an hourglass. If heaven's throne room has a calendar, one day is circled in red and highlighted in yellow. God has decreed a family reunion:

> The Master himself will give the command. Archangel thunder! God's trumpet blast! He'll come down from

heaven and the dead in Christ will rise—they'll go first. Then the rest of us who are still alive at the time will be caught up with them into the clouds to meet the Master. Oh, we'll be walking on air! And then there will be one huge family reunion with the Master. (1 Thessalonians 4:16–18 MSG)

Lᴏʀᴅ, God of Israel, . . . only you are God of all the kingdoms of the earth. You made the heavens and the earth. * I have no one in heaven but you; I want nothing on earth besides you. * The Lᴏʀᴅ has set his throne in heaven, and his kingdom rules over everything. * I heard a loud voice from the throne, saying, "Now God's presence is with people, and he will live with them, and they will be his people. God himself will be with them and will be their God."

2 KINGS 19:15; PSALM 73:25; PSALM
103:19; REVELATION 21:3

TRUST
GOD TO
TRIUMPH

GOD SEES YOUR TEARS

A couple of days ago, twenty thousand of us ran through the streets of San Antonio raising money for breast cancer research. Most of us ran out of kindness, happy to log three miles and donate a few dollars to the cause. A few ran in memory of a loved one; others, in honor of a cancer survivor. We ran for different reasons. But no runner was more passionate than one I spotted. A bandanna covered her bald head, and dark circles shadowed her eyes. She had cancer. While we ran out of kindness, she ran out of conviction. She knows how cancer victims feel. She's been there.

The phrase "I've been there" is in the chorus of Christ's theme song. To the lonely, Jesus whispers, "I've been there." To the discouraged, Christ nods his head and sighs, "I've been there."

Jesus has been there. He experienced "all the pain, all the testing" (Hebrews 2:18, MSG). Jesus was angry enough to purge the temple, hungry enough to eat raw grain, and distraught enough to weep in public.

Whatever you are facing, he knows how you feel.[11]

You look at tomorrow's demands, next week's bills,

next month's silent calendar. Your future looks as barren as the Sinai Desert. "How can I face my future?"

God knows what you need and where you'll be. Trust him. Fretting over tomorrow's problems today siphons the strength you need for now, leaving you anemic and weak.[12]

Can I share some suggestions to help you get through difficult days?

1. Meet your fears with faith.

Do what my father urged my brother and me to do. Summertime for the Lucado family always involved a trip from West Texas to the Rocky Mountains. My dad loved to fish for trout on the edge of the white-water rivers. Yet he knew that the currents were dangerous and his sons could be careless. Upon arrival we'd scout out the safe places to cross the river. He'd walk us down the bank until we found a line of stable rocks. He was even known to add one or two to compensate for our short strides.

As we watched, he'd test the stones, knowing if they held him, they'd hold us. Once on the other side, he'd signal for us to follow.

"Don't be afraid," he could have said. "Trust me."

Does a river of fear run between you and Jesus? Cross over to him.

Believe he can. Believe he cares.[13]

2. Go back to the Bible stories.

Read them again and again. Be reminded that you aren't the first person to weep. And you aren't the first person to be helped.

Read the story and remember, their story is yours!

The challenge too great? Read the story. That's you crossing the Red Sea with Moses.

Too many worries? Read the story. That's you receiving heavenly food with the Israelites.

Your wounds too deep? Read the story. That's you, Joseph, forgiving your brothers for betraying you.[14]

3. Stir the pot of prayer.

Let's say a stress stirrer comes your way. The doctor decides you need an operation. She detects a lump and thinks it best that you have it removed. So there you are, walking out of her office. You've just been handed this cup of anxiety. What are you going to do with it? You can place it in one of two pots.

You can dump your bad news in the vat of worry and pull out the spoon. Turn on the fire. Stew on it. Stir it. Mope for a while. Brood for a time. Won't be long before you'll have a delightful pot of pessimism.

How about a different idea? The pot of prayer. Before the door of the doctor's office closes, give the problem to God. "I receive your lordship. Nothing comes to me that hasn't passed through you."

Your part is prayer and gratitude.

God's part? Peace. "You will experience God's peace, which exceeds anything we can understand. His peace will guard your hearts and minds as you live in Christ Jesus" (Philippians 4:7 NLT).[15]

Finally, I want to encourage you to remember that God is involved in your life. He will take care of you. Why is it important to remember this? Because knowing that God is in charge counterbalances the mystery of why and how.

God is plotting for our good. In all the setbacks and slipups, he is ordaining the best for our future. Every event of our day is designed to draw us toward our God and our destiny.

"[God] works out everything in conformity with the purpose of his will" (Ephesians 1:11 NIV). *Everything* means everything. No exceptions.

He will carry you through.

Lᴏʀᴅ my God, you have done many miracles.
Your plans for us are many.
If I tried to tell them all,
there would be too many to count.

PSALM 40:5

Do you believe that no evil is beyond God's reach? That he can redeem every pit, including this one in which you find yourself?

What if Joseph had given up on God? At any point along his broken road, he could have turned sour and walked away. "No more. No more. I'm out."

You can give up on God as well. The cemetery of hope is overpopulated with sour souls who have settled for a small God. Don't be among them.

In Her Own Words:
JULIE'S STORY

I grew up in an ideal but not perfect home. My family loved and served God, but my heart was not in a right place. When I was sixteen, my dad died suddenly from a brain aneurysm. My grief was so intense. God was faithful: he comforted and provided for my family in so many ways. Still, my heart was not his.

I became depressed, and that depression led to an eating disorder. My life was falling apart, and I felt like the only thing I could control was my weight. I became bulimic.

I thought I had my eating disorder under control—until I woke up one day and realized I couldn't stop making myself throw up. I wasn't even sure I wanted to stop. My mind became so dark, and I felt bad about myself. Yet God was there with me.

My heavenly Father called out to me in my darkness. I confessed my sin to him and to my mom. She became both my accountability partner and my prayer partner. God himself showed me that the only way I could get out of this pit was to let his truth clean out my mind. I was so desperate for his Word. I carried verses on note cards everywhere I went. When a destructive thought entered my mind, I pulled out a truth from God's Word and spoke it out loud. With that initial step, I slowly began to see myself the way God sees me.

By God's power at work in me, I learned that he delights in me. That he dances over me. That he is head over heels in love with me. I have also learned that Jesus took me by the hand and delivered me from the pit. God gave me so many chances that I didn't deserve. He is always faithful, and he is always full of unfailing love and compassion. That was ten years ago. Praise God! I have never been freer than I am in him. He has my whole heart.

People, trust God all the time. Tell him all your problems, because God is our protection. * "I am the LORD your God, who teaches you to do what is good, who leads you in the way you should go." * The LORD is good to everyone; he is merciful to all he has made. * You have recorded my troubles. You have kept a list of my tears. * "Don't be afraid, because I have saved you. I have called you by name, and you are mine." * You go before me and follow me. You place your hand of blessing on my head. * Those who know the LORD trust him, because he will not leave those who come to him.

PSALM 62:8; ISAIAH 48:17; PSALM 145:9; PSALM 56:8; ISAIAH 43:1; PSALM 139:5 NLT; PSALM 9:10

I don't have an easy solution or a magic wand. I have found something—Someone—far better. God himself.

ULTIMATE VICTORY

That you may know what is the hope of His calling, what
are the riches of the glory of His inheritance in the saints,
and what is the exceeding greatness of His power toward
us who believe, according to the working of His mighty
power which He worked in Christ when He raised Him
from the dead and seated Him at His right hand in the
heavenly places, far above all principality and power and
might and dominion, and every name that is named, not
only in this age but also in that which is to come.

EPHESIANS 1:18–21 NKJV

Life turns every person upside down. No one escapes unscathed. Not the woman who discovers her husband is having an affair. Not the businessman who has his investments embezzled by a crooked colleague. Not the teenager who discovers that a night of romance has resulted in a surprise pregnancy. Not the pastor who feels his faith shaken by questions of suffering and fear.

We'd be foolish to think we are invulnerable.

But we'd be just as foolish to think that evil wins the day.

The Bible vibrates with the steady drumbeat of faith: God recycles evil into righteousness. Perhaps you read this book in search of a quick fix for your challenges. "How to

Overcome Obstacles in Five Easy Steps." Sorry to disappoint. I don't have an easy solution or a magic wand. I have found something—Someone—far better. God himself. When God gets in the middle of life, evil becomes good.

Haven't we seen this discovery in the story of Joseph? Saddled with setbacks: family rejection, deportation, slavery, and imprisonment. Yet he emerged triumphant, a hero of his generation. Among his final recorded words are these comments to his brothers: "You meant evil against me; but God meant it for good" (Genesis 50:20 NKJV).

This is the repeated pattern in Scripture. *Evil. God. Good.*

See the cross on the hill? Can you hear the soldiers pound the nails? Jesus' enemies smirk. Satan's demons lurk. All that is evil rubs its hands in glee. "This time," Satan whispers. "This time I will win."

For a silent Saturday it appeared he did. The final breath. The battered body. Mary wept. Blood seeped down the timber into the dirt. Followers lowered God's Son as the sun set. Soldiers sealed the tomb, and night fell over the earth.

Yet what Satan intended as the ultimate evil, God used for the ultimate good. God rolled the rock away. Jesus walked out on Sunday morning, a smile on his face and a bounce to his step. And if you look closely, you see Satan scampering from the cemetery with his forked tail between his legs.

"Will I ever win?" he grumbles.

No. He won't.

God will
carry you
through.

ENDNOTES

1. Spiros Zodhiates, ed., *The Hebrew-Greek Key Word Study Bible: Key Insights into God's Word, New American Standard Bible*, rev. ed. (Chattanooga, TN: AMG, 2008), Genesis 50:20. See also "Greek/Hebrew Definitions," Bible Tools, Strong's #2803, *chashab*, www.bibletools.org/index.cfm/fuseaction/Lexicon.show/ID/H2803/chashab.htm.
2. "Every shepherd is an abomination to the Egyptians" (Gen. 46:34).
3. Howard Rutledge and Phyllis Rutledge with Mel White and Lyla White, *In the Presence of Mine Enemies—1965–1973: A Prisoner of War* (New York: Fleming H. Revell, 1975), 33, 35.
4. Rutledge and Rutledge, *In the Presence*, 39, 52.
5. "Spite House," New York Architecture Images, nyc-architecture.com, http://nyc-architecture.com/GON/GON005.htm.
6. Rick Reilly, "Matt Steven Can't See the Hoop. But He'll Still Take the Last Shot," Life of Reilly, ESPN.com, March 11, 2009, http://sports.espn.go.com/espnmag/story?id=3967807. See also Gil Spencer, "Blind Player Helps Team See the Value of Sportsmanship," *Delaware County Daily Times*, February 25, 2009, www.delcotimes.com/articles/2009/02/25/sports/doc49a4c50632d09134430615.
7. "The Story of Keep Calm and Carry On," YouTube video, 3:01, posted by Temujin Doran, www.youtube.com/watch?v=FrHkKXFRbCI&sns=fb. See also *Keep Calm and Carry On: Good Advice for Hard Times* (Kansas City, MO: Andrews McMeel, 2009), introduction.
8. Jim Collins, "How to Manage Through Chaos," CNN Money, September 30, 2011, http://management.fortune.cnn.com/2011/09/30/jim-collins-great-by-choice-exclusive-excerpt.
9. Ibid.
10. Todd Burpo with Lynn Vincent, *Heaven Is for Real: A Little Boy's Astounding Story of His Trip to Heaven and Back* (Nashville: Thomas Nelson, 2011), 94–96.
11. Max Lucado, *Next Door Savior* (Nashville: W Publishing Group, 2003), 13, 16.
12. Max Lucado, *Every Day Deserves a Chance* (Nashville: Thomas Nelson, Inc., 2007), 53–54.
13. Ibid, 88.
14. Max Lucado, *He Still Moves Stones* (Nashville: W Publishing Group, 1993), 91.
15. Max Lucado, *Come Thirsty* (Nashville: Thomas Nelson, Inc., 2004), 105.

IF YOU HAVE ENJOYED THIS BOOK
OR IT HAS TOUCHED YOUR LIFE IN SOME WAY,
WE WOULD LOVE TO HEAR FROM YOU.

Please send your comments to:
Hallmark Book Feedback
P.O. Box 419034
Mail Drop 100
Kansas City, MO 64141

Or e-mail us at:
booknotes@hallmark.com